INSTANT POT COOKBOOK FOR TWO

550 Amazingly Easy & Delicious Instant Pot Recipes to Enjoy Together

BY

Francis Michael

ISBN: 978-1-952504-28-0

COPYRIGHT © 2020 by Francis Michael

All rights reserved. This book is copyright protected and it's for personal use only. Without the prior written permission of the publisher, no part of this publication should be reproduced, distributed, or transmitted in any form or by any means, including photocopying, recording, or other electronic or mechanical methods. This publication is sold with the idea that the publisher is not required to render accounting, officially permitted, or otherwise, qualified services. Seek for the services of a legal or professional, a practiced individual in the profession if advice is needed.

DISCLAIMER

The information contained in this book is geared for educational and entertainment purposes only. Concerted efforts have been made towards providing accurate, up to date and reliable complete information. The information in this book is true and complete to the best of our knowledge. Neither the publisher nor the author takes any responsibility for any possible consequences of reading or enjoying the recipes in this book. The author and publisher disclaim any liability in connection with the use of information contained in this book. Under no circumstance will any legal responsibility or blame be apportioned against the author or publisher for any reparation, damages, or monetary loss due to the information herein, either directly or indirectly.

Chocolate Lava Cake

Preparation time: 5 minutes

Cook time: 30 minutes

Total time: 35 minutes

Servings: 2

Calories: 560kcal

Ingredients:

- 0.5 tablespoon of granulated sugar
- 0.25 cup of butter, cut into pieces
- 2 oz. semisweet chocolate, chopped
- 0.5 cup of confectioners' sugar
- 1 eggs
- 1 egg yolks
- 0.5 teaspoon of instant coffee granules
- 0.5 teaspoon of vanilla extract
- 3 tablespoons of all-purpose flour
- 0.13 teaspoon of salt

Cooking Instructions:

1. Grease the bottom of four 6 ounces of ramekins and coat each ramekin with sugar. Melt the chocolate and butter.
2. Microwave the butter and chocolate in a micro wave on medium heat for about 1 minute. Stir and continue heating at 15-second intervals, until the chocolate is melted and smooth.
3. Continue stirring to melt the chocolate completely in the residual heat. Stir in confectioner's sugar. Then, whisk in eggs, yolks, coffee and vanilla.
4. Stir in flour and salt and divide batter among each of the ramekins. Add 1 cup of water into the bottom of your Instant Pot and place the trivet inside.

5. Place 3 ramekins on the trivet and add 1 more ramekin on top. Close and lock the lid in place. Select Manual, High Pressure for about 7 to 9 minutes.
6. When the timer beeps, do a quick pressure release. Carefully open the lid and remove the ramekin. Dust the chocolate lava cakes with powdered sugar.
7. Serve hot and enjoy!

Table of Contents

INTRODUCTION 8
Meaning of Instant Pot 8
Benefits of Cooking with Instant Pot 9
Function Keys of Your Instant Pot 11
How to Clean Your Instant Pot 14

BREAKFAST MEALS 16
Breakfast Porridge 16
Apple Cinnamon Steel Cut Oats 18
Mashed Potatoes 19
Pumpkin Pie Oatmeal 20
Instant Pot Barley 21
Jamaican Cornmeal Porridge 22
Mac and Cheese 23
Creamy Grits with Cheddar and Jalapeño 24
Cinnamon Crunch Oatmeal 25
Instant Pot Spaghetti 27
Peaches and Cream Oatmeal 29
Mexican Breakfast Casserole 30
Sweet Potatoes 32

POULTRY MEALS 33
Creamy Mushroom and Chicken Wild Rice Stew 33
Chicken and Dumplings 34
Chicken Stock 36
Asian Sesame Chicken 37
Butter Chicken 39

Honey Garlic Chicken 41

Creamy Chicken Tortellini Soup 43

Turkey Chili 45

Chicken and Rice 47

Salsa Chicken 49

Chicken Spaghetti 51

SOUP MEALS 53

Jalapeño Lime Chicken Soup 53

Minestrone Soup 55

Harvest Butternut Squash Soup 56

Sausage and Herbed White Bean Soup 57

Mexican Tortilla Soup 58

Curried Coconut Lentil Soup 60

Moroccan Spiced Soup 61

Lentil Soup with Sausage 63

SEA FOOD MEALS 65

Shrimp Paella 65

Cajun Dirty Rice 67

Salmon with Creamy Herb Parmesan Sauce 69

Sweet and Spicy Pineapple Shrimp 70

Creamy Shrimp Scampi 71

Shrimp Risotto 73

Crustless Crab Quiche 74

Shrimp Coconut Curry 76

Shrimp Scampi Paella 77

Salmon with Chili-Lime Sauce 79

Salmon, Broccoli & Potatoes 81

Lemon Pepper Salmon 82

BEEF MEALS 84

Beef and Broccoli 84

Beef Tips and Gravy with Mashed Potatoes 86

Cubed Steak and Gravy 88

Beef Stroganoff 89

Chili Lime Short Ribs 91

Sloppy Joes 93

Beef Vindaloo 95

Braised Korean Beef Ragu 97

Beef Curry 99

Braised Brisket 101

Spicy Orange Beef 103

Ethiopian Beef Stew 105

STEW MEALS 107

Brunswick Stew 107

White Bean, Chickpea, and Tomato Stew 109

Tortilla Chicken Verde Chili 111

Italian Sausage Stew 113

Chicken & Smoked Sausage Stew 115

Chocolatey Beef Stew 117

Butter Chicken Curry 118

Beef Masala Curry 120

Venison Stew 122

Kimchi Stew 124

PORK MEALS 126

   Pork Poblano Skillet Enchiladas 126

   Pork Chops with Gravy 128

   Baby Back Pork Ribs 130

   Ginger Pork Shogayaki 132

   Bacon Wrapped Pork 134

   Cafe Rio Pork 136

   Sausage Gravy 138

   Pulled Pork 139

   Honey Soy Pork Tenderloin 141

   Pork Chile Verde 142

   Kalua Pork 144

   Boneless Pork Chops 145

VEGETARIAN MEALS 147

   Thai Butternut Squash Curry 147

   Vegetable Soup 149

   Mashed Sweet Potatoes with Garlic and Rosemary 151

   Creamy Broccoli Mac and Cheese 153

   Steamed Artichokes 154

   Cheesy Garlic Spaghetti Squash 155

   Spiced Quinoa and Cauliflower Rice Bowls 156

   Portobello Pot Roast 158

   Vegetarian Chili 160

VEGAN MEALS 162

   Mushroom Risotto 162

Lentil Coconut Curry 164

Quinoa Burrito Bowls 166

Cauliflower Tikka Masala 168

Vegan Sloppy Joes 170

Cilantro Lime Quinoa 172

Vegan Alfredo Sauce 173

Maple Bourbon Chili 174

Vegan Mashed Potatoes 176

DESSERT MEALS 178

Applesauce 178

Buttered Cabbage 179

Egg Bites 180

Carrot Cake Cheesecake 181

Garlic Noodles 183

Arroz Con Leche 185

Apple Cake 186

Pumpkin Pie Pudding 188

Chocolate Lava Cake 189

INTRODUCTION

Meaning of Instant Pot

The Instant Pot is an electronic cooking device or machine programmed to perform the function of 7 gadgets. Unlike electric pressure cooker, steamer, slow cooker, yoghurt maker, rice cooker, warming pot or sauté pan, Instant Pot is a cooker programmed with multi-functions which can perform the same task like the afore mentioned machines. The Instant Pot is a seven-in-one multi cooker combined that can work as an electric pressure cooker, steamer, slow cooker, yoghurt maker, rice cooker, and sauté pan. It can cook meals instantly and faster but it has an option for a start time that can be programmed to delay.

Some people that likes convenient cooking and the option of "set it and forget it" in a slow cooker would have a great passion for Instant Pot and also including those who desires to have a pressure cooker, steamer, yoghurt maker and slow cooker simultaneously but has little or no space to occupy the four cookers, Instant Pot performs the same functions like the other four machines. The Instant Pot comes with instruction manual and short booklet of recipes which contain functions of Instant Pot and manufacturer's recommended quantities of food ingredients together with preparation and cooking times to help the newbies.

The Instant Pot will save you a whole lots of time if you wants to cook food like stew, lentils or grains. The special thing about Instant Pot is that it has a lot of functional uses for a single appliance and you can set it and walk away doing other things while the machine does its magic. With its multi-functional ability, it may seem difficult to operate your Instant Pot but it's very easy to operate when you follow the instruction manual.

Benefits of Cooking with Instant Pot

1. It Can Cook Beans Super-Fast.

This reason alone got my attention to this fabulous Instant Pot device. While it takes some people about 12-15 minutes to cook soaked beans and 37-40 minutes to cook dry beans. I was not fully convinced when the Instant Pot cook beans very fast until I heard it over and over again from different people and their good comments made about their Instant Pot. That was when I started having great passion for Instant Pot and it earned a space in my kitchen.

2. To Make Perfect Brown Rice.

It's not easy to cook brown rice but it was easy for me. I have been thinking brown rice was easy to cook but was doubtful the first time I cooked brown rice with little water and I thought I would made crunchy rice. However, the rice was not crunchy as I thought and it was perfect rice I have ever cooked. You can use your Instant Pot to make recipes like Mexican Casserole, Cheesy Broccoli and Rice Casserole perfectly in a fraction of the time.

3. Steam/Cook Veggies in Minutes.

The Instant Pot cooks veggies in minutes. When cooking veggies, do not walk away to avoid burning or overcooking your veggies. It's important to stick to the step by step recipes instructions when cooking veggies. I've burned more than my fair share of veggies by forgetting about them. You have to make use of quick pressure release to release the steam once they are finished cooking.

4. Built in Timer.

What amazes me the most about the Instant Pot machine is the fact that you can cook a meal, walk away and come back later to meet fully cooked meals. The Instant Pot will not start cooking by itself until you want it to cook by using the timer. You can program your dinner to start at 4:30pm and keep it warm until you get home.

5. Easy Clean Up.

Washing of my dishes is one of the things I have little time to do. I do avoid cooking dishes that will require thorough washing of dishes. When it comes to Instant Pot, it is very easy to clean up after use.

6. Pressure Cooking Retains More Nutrients.

Researchers have it that food cooked for a short time with less water retains more nutrients. Instant Pot retains more nutrients because of its short duration used for cooking. Due to the high pressure, beans and grains become more digestible.

7. They are Safe.

There are some reports on injuries or dangers of pressure cookers blowing up while cooking. Some people became scared of using pressure cooker because of some domestic violence caused by the pressure cooker. However, Instant Pot is very safe to use. It has 10 in-built safety features which include high temperature warning, a lid which is to be locked while cooking, automatic pressure control and many others.

8. Slow Cooker.

The Instant Pot is a little taller but has the same size with slow cookers. The Instant Pot also perform the function of a slow cooker by just pressing a button. Some people may decide to use their Instant Pot as a slow cooker on regular bases. By doing this, you must make sure you buy the optional lid so you can be able to use the Instant Pot as a slow cooker on regular basis.

9. Sauté feature.

The Instant Pot has a sauté feature. It means the Instant Pot can also perform the function of a sauté pan. So you can toss onions and garlic in, select sauté button, prepare the rest of your ingredients and then add them to the pot and set the time you want Instant Pot to cook whatever you wants to cook.

Function Keys of Your Instant Pot

1. **Manual / Pressure Buttons:**

    This function will be frequently used which enables you to select the cooking time manually and pressure cook what you wants to cook. The Instant Pot pressure, time and temperature can be adjusted by pressing the "+/-" features. It is imperative to follow the recipe instructions to know if you are to pressure cook the food using Low or High Pressure. The "Manual" and "Pressure" button stands for pressure cooking unlike functions like "Sauté", "Yogurt" or "Slow cooker" which does not require pressure cooking. The Instant Pot's default setting is High Pressure when you press the "Manual" button.

2. **Sauté Button:**

    This feature is the second most frequently used button on the Instant Pot. You can select the sauté button to cook up anything as you would in a skillet or pan without 1 cup of liquid. All you need to do is just to set the "Sauté" button, add some cooking oil like butter, avocado, coconut or animal fat like beef tallow or lard to the inner pot and add food you want to cook like a skillet or pan. The sauté button can be used to cook ingredients like onion, garlic and meat. Most times, I start with the "Sauté" function and then use the "Manual" / "Pressure" button to pressure cook my meal.

3. **Slow Cook Button:**

    This button helps you to use Instant Pot like a slower cooker. This function allows the Instant Pot to perform the function of a slow cooker. Just add food as you normally do to a slow cooker, secure the lid and then select the "Slow Cook" button and use "+/-" buttons to adjust the cook time.

4. **Bean / Chili:**

    This button allows the Instant Pot to cook beans faster than any other cooker. This is why beans is the food I like cooking most in my Instant Pot. The "Bean / Chili" button, uses the default High Pressure for 30 minutes though it can be adjusted for "More" to High Pressure for 35 minutes or "Less" for High Pressure for 20 minutes. Black beans take about 10-15 minutes, while kidney beans take 20-25. The Instant Pot Manual has different cooking times for various beans and legumes.

5. **Meat / Stew:**

    The Instant Pot can easily make your favorite stew or meat dish. It can make it by adjusting the settings depending on the desired texture. For instance, a homemade stew with about 1-2 lb. of meat, you can set it to "Meat / Stew" button using high pressure for

    35 minutes. The "More" setting is great for fall-off-the-bone cooking. It will set to a default High Pressure for 35 minutes. The Instant Pot can be adjusted for "More" to High Pressure for 45 minutes or "Less" for High Pressure for 20 minutes.

6. **Multigrain:**

This function can be used for cooking wild rice or brown rice which usually takes longer time than cooking white rice. Cook brown rice to a 1:1.25 ratio rice to water and wild rice to a 1:3 ratio rice to water for 25-30 minutes. The default (Normal) setting is 40 minutes of cooking time but can be adjusted as required for the "Less" setting to 20 minutes of cooking time, or "More" at 45 minutes of warm water soaking and 60 minutes of cooking.

7. **Porridge:**

Rice porridge (congee) and other grains can be cooked using the porridge button.

The default cooking time on High Pressure for rice porridge is 20 minutes but can be adjusted for "More" to High Pressure for 30 minutes or "Less" for High Pressure for 15 minutes. When the cooking cycle has completed, it is not advisable to use Quick Pressure Release because it has high starch content and may splatter the porridge through the steam release vent. It's imperative to use the Natural Pressure Release to release the steam.

8. **Poultry:**

This button can be used for making chicken and other poultry recipes in the Instant Pot. The default cooking program is 15 minutes but can be adjusted for "More" to High Pressure for 30 minutes or "Less" for High Pressure for 5 minutes. I always make shredded chicken for homemade tacos and burrito bowls. Add about 1 lb. uncooked chicken, ¼ cup of homemade salsa, 1 cup of bone broth, 1 tsp. cumin, 1 clove garlic minced, ½ tsp oregano, ½ onion, and $^{1/8}$ tsp. paprika into the bottom of your Instant Pot. Secure the lid in place and select the "Poultry" button to the default at High Pressure for 15 minutes. When the cooking cycle has finished, do a Natural Pressure Release for 10 minutes. Carefully open the lid, shred the chicken the two forks, add pepper and salt to taste.

9. **Rice:**

This button is used to cook rice in your Instant Pot using half the time a conventional rice cooker could use. It uses about 4 to 8 minutes, short grain, Jasmine, White rice, and Basmati rice can all be cooked using this function. You'll need a 1:1 ratio of rice to water (Basmati is a 1:1.5 ratio). It depends on the quantity of food you want to cook on low pressure, when you press the "Rice" button, the cooking duration automatically adjusts. It's always necessary to add further 10-12 minutes to the cooking time to allow the Instant Pot to come to pressure but cooking rice in the "Manual" mode at high pressure is my frequent selection. I usually add 1:1 ratio of rice to water into the bottom of my Instant Pot and set to 3 minutes with a 12 minute Natural Pressure Release when the timer beeps..

10. **Soup:**

Soup, stock, and broth can be made using the "Soup" button. Water doesn't heavily boil because Instant Pot will control the pressure and temperature so that the liquid doesn't heavily boil. You can adjust the cooking time as required, usually between 20-40 minutes, and the pressure to either Low or High Pressure. Anytime you wish to make homemade bone broth faster than the conventional slow cooker, it is very simple. Click the "Soup" button, set the Low Pressure, and set the cooking time to 120 minutes. Once the timer beeps, do Natural Pressure Release to release the steam.

11. **Steam:**

This button can be used to steam vegetables, seafood or reheat food. Always use the steam rack of your Instant Pot when steaming veggies to avoid burning and sticking to the bottom of your Instant Pot. Add 1-2 cups of water to the inner liner, place the steam rack inside the inner pot and with a stainless steel steam basket on top. Add the vegetables, seafood, etc. in the basket. Select the "Steam" button and then adjust the time using the "+" or "-" key. When you are cooking foods like frozen corn on the cob or a fresh fish filet, adjust the time to 3-5 minutes and 8-10 minutes if you are cooking fresh artichokes could take 9-11 minutes.

12. **Keep Warm Button:**

This button is used to keep food hot when the Instant Pot is done with cooking or to cancel the pressure cooking mode. Immediately cooking time is finished, the Instant Pot will beep and automatically go into the "Keep Warm" function. It will display an "L" in front of a number to indicate how long it's been warm – e.g. "L0:30" for 30 minutes. This button helps to keep food warm (145 to 172°F) for up to 99 hours, 50 minutes.

13. **Cancel Button:**

If by mistake you selected wrong cooking time and you want to stop cooking or adjust pressure cooking time, you can cancel and return to standby mode by selecting the "Keep Warm" / "Cancel" button.

14. **Timer Button:**

This button can be used to delay the cooking start time for the Instant Pot for both pressure cooking and slow cook options. Press the Timer button with 10 seconds of pressing Pressure / Manual button or Slow Cook button. To adjust the delayed hours, Use "+/-" buttons then wait a second and press Timer again to set delayed minutes. Press the Keep Warm / Cancel button to cancel the Timer anytime.

How to Clean Your Instant Pot

Step 1: Unplug

Before you start cleaning your Instant Pot, make sure it is unplugged. It's advisable to unplug your Instant Pot whenever it's not in use. For this purpose, you have to make sure it's unplugged for the intensive cleaning you're about to do, for the safety of your Instant Pot and for your safety too.

Step 2: Cleaning housing unit

The outside housing unit cannot go into the dishwasher so you should be able to clean it thoroughly with a rag. Get the rag good and damp with water and cleaning solution, and wipe down both the interior and exterior parts of the main housing unit. To have a perfect cleaning, a sponge is recommended to get those hard or stiff food bits and mineral deposits. Don't fail to clean everywhere you may have tiny particles.

Step 3: Wash the lid

The lid has to be washed properly. This can be done by washing it in the sink with warm water with a little dish soap to make all the residuals are removed because this can contaminate. Some people used a vinegar solution to remove the unpleasant smell from residuals.

Step 4: Check other crevices

There are some parts in the Instant Pot that you might not like to cleaning all the time you are washing the Instant Pot. Get all those crevices and small parts where food residue may build up for some period of time. Remove the Quick Release handle, and wash it with warm-soapy water. In some cases, the steam valve can get blocked if too much deposit builds up there. Remove the shield, located inside the lid which blocks the valve. The shield could pop off easily depending on the model your Instant Pot. Wash the shield in the sink. Check the condensation collection cup at the side of your Instant Pot. It might have collected food residue over time. If it has some residue on it, clean it in the sink.

Step 5: clean sealing ring

The silicone ring found on the underside of the lid will likely need a thorough cleaning. This is what indicates your Instant Pot has a tight seal, and it's an easy spot for food particles or residual smells to lurk. Check it for any signs of damage, as silicone can start to crack over time. If you notice any crack in the silicone ring, it has been damaged and needs a replacement immediately. The silicone ring is dishwasher-safe, so you can pop it in there on the top rack. Once it's thoroughly cleaned, place it back on the underside of the lid, and make sure you've got a secure fit.

Step 6: Wash the inner pot

The inner pot is dishwasher-safe. With this fact, you should be washing the inner pot at regularly intervals. Since you're doing a deep clean, it doesn't hurt to pop the inner pot into the dishwasher together with any of the other dishwasher-safe parts you use with your Instant Pot, such as silicone molds and wire racks. When you finished washing the inner pot, dry it off using a paper towel or use some household vinegar to give it a thorough wipe-down. By doing this, it can get rid of any accumulated residue from things like minerals in your water, or dish detergent. This will make your Instant Pot looks shiny and nice.

Step 7: Steam clean and let dry

At this stage, you have done a thorough cleaning, reassemble all the parts. Don't forget about those small parts like the sealing ring and shield because they can be missed easily. The purpose of this washing and cleaning is to ensure your Instant Pot is safe so you can use it for a long period of time. However, after doing all the washing and cleaning but you realized the sealing ring still has a strange food smell, you may need to deodorize the part with a vinegar steam clean. The process is simple and can be done directly in the Instant Pot by adding a cup of water, a cup of vinegar, and some lemon peels (for extra freshness!) to the inner pot, press "Steam" button and set for a few minutes. When the timer beeps, do a natural pressure release. Open the lid, remove the sealing ring and dry it at a convenient place.

BREAKFAST MEALS

Breakfast Porridge

Preparation time: 5 minutes

Cook time: 15 minutes

Total time: 20 minutes

Serves: 2

Ingredients:

- 2–3 tablespoons of lightly toasted sunflower seeds or 1 tablespoon of tahini
- 2 tablespoons of unsweetened shredded coconut
- 1 tablespoon of chia seed or flaxseed
- ½ teaspoon of cinnamon
- 1 teaspoon of ginger, ground
- A pinch of turmeric, ground
- A pinch of sea salt
- ½ cup of water or coconut milk
- 1 cup of squash, peeled and chopped into large pieces
- Hemp protein or collagen, optional
- Pure maple syrup or raw honey
- For toppings: tart cherries (pitted), blueberries, pomegranate seeds, sesame seed, and/or coconut cream or yogurt to top.

Cooking Instructions:

1. Add the squash into in the Instant Pot with 1 tablespoon of coconut oil. Add in a pinch of cinnamon and nutmeg.

2. Press the Sauté function and cook for 5 minutes, turning the squash. Add 1/3 cup of water when the squash is coated.
3. Close and lock the lid in place. Select Manual, High Pressure for 6 minutes. When the timer beeps, do a natural pressure release for about 10 minutes.
4. Remove the lid and drain the water. Puree the squash with a hand blender. Mix in the remaining ingredients like dry mix and tahini/sesame mix and a splash of milk.
5. Give everything a good stir. Lock the lid in place and keep it on warm mode until ready to serve.
6. Serve and enjoy!

Apple Cinnamon Steel Cut Oats

Preparation time: 5 minutes

Cook time: 25 minutes

Total time: 30 minutes

Servings: 2

Ingredients:

- 1 cups of steel cut oats
- 2 ½ cups of water or non-dairy milk
- 1 medium apple, diced
- 1 tsp. of brown sugar (optional)
- 1 tsp. of cinnamon
- 1 cinnamon sticks
- 1/8 tsp. of nutmeg

Cooking Instructions:

1. Add all the ingredients into the bottom of your Instant Pot and give everything a good stir to combine.
2. Close and lock the lid. Select Manual, High Pressure for 4 minutes. When the timer beeps, do a natural pressure release for about 10 minutes.
3. Carefully open the lid and stir the oatmeal. Top with additional cinnamon and diced apple. Add a splash of milk if desired.
4. Serve and enjoy!

Mashed Potatoes

Preparation time: 15 minutes

Cook time: 15 minutes

Total time: 30 minutes

Serves: 2

Ingredients:

- 2 lb. of Russet potatoes (about 4 medium potatoes), peeled and sliced into 5 or 6 big slices
- 1 clove garlic, peeled and smashed
- ½ tsp. of salt
- ½ cup of milk
- 3 tbsp. of unsalted butter, plus more for serving
- 2 oz. of cream cheese
- Freshly ground black pepper
- Chopped fresh parsley, optional

Cooking Instructions:

1. Add the sliced potatoes into the bottom of your Instant Pot with 2 cups of cold water. Add the garlic clove and salt.
2. Close and lock the lid. Select Manual, High Pressure for 8 minutes. When the timer beeps, do a quick pressure release.
3. Carefully open the lid and drain any excess water. Pour the potatoes into a strainer to drain out the water. Add the potatoes back in the pot.
4. Then, chop the butter and cream cheese into cubes. Add them in a microwave-safe dish, pour the milk on top, and heat for about 30 seconds in the microwave.
5. Pour the milk, butter and cream cheese mixture on top of the potatoes. Mash the potatoes with a non-metal potato masher and incorporate everything together.
6. Adjust the seasoning with more salt and freshly ground black pepper.
7. Serve with chopped fresh parsley and extra pats of butter on top.

Pumpkin Pie Oatmeal

Preparation time: 5 minutes

Cook time: 13 minutes

Total time: 23 minutes

Servings: 2

Calories: 326kcal

Ingredients:

- 1 cup of water, divided
- 1 cups of rolled old fashioned oats
- 0.88 cup of milk 2%
- 0.25 cup of pumpkin puree
- 0.5 teaspoon of pumpkin pie spice
- 0.13 teaspoon of vanilla extract
- 0.25 cup of maple syrup
- Chopped pecans, for topping

Cooking Instructions:

1. Add 1 cup of water into the bottom of your Instant Pot. Press the Sauté function to boil the water.
2. Place the oats, 1 cup of water, milk, pumpkin puree, pumpkin pie spice, vanilla extract, and maple syrup to steamer insert. Give everything a good stir.
3. Cover the steamer insert. Press the Cancel function on the Instant Pot and add the covered steamer insert into the pot.
4. Close and lock the lid. Select Manual, High Pressure for 8 minutes. When the timer beeps, do a natural pressure release for about 5 minutes, then quick release any remaining pressure.
5. Carefully open the lid and remove the oatmeal from pot. Give everything a good stir and top with chopped pecans.
6. Serve and enjoy!

Instant Pot Barley

Servings: 2

Preparation time: 10 minutes

Cook time: 18 minutes

Total time: 28 minutes

Ingredients:

- ½ tbsp. of olive oil
- ½ cup of pearl barley
- ¼ cup of red or sweet onion, finely chopped
- 2 cups of liquid, We used half broth and half water
- ½ tsp. of sea salt
- 2 oz. of turkey ham, diced (optional)
- 2 oz. of baby kale, or baby greens
- 2 eggs, cooked to your preference

Cooking Instructions:

1. Press the Sauté function on the Instant Pot and add the olive oil. Add the barley, onion and cook until it smells toasty.
2. Add the liquid and salt. Close and lock the lid. Select Manual, High Pressure for 18 minutes. While the barley cooks, dice the ham (if desired).
3. When the timer beeps, do a quick pressure release. Press the Sauté function and add the diced ham if desired. Cook, stirring occasionally while preparing the eggs.
4. Once the eggs are ready, add the arugula to the pot, and give everything a good stir to combine. Scoop the barley mixture into individual plates.
5. Top with an egg cooked to your preference. Garnish with Aleppo pepper, fresh ground pepper, fresh herbs, scallions, etc.
6. Serve immediately and enjoy!

Jamaican Cornmeal Porridge

Preparation time: 5 minutes

Cook time: 20 minutes

Total time: 25 minutes

Servings: 2

Calories: 241kcal

Ingredients:

- 2 cups of water, divided
- 0.5 cup of milk
- 0.5 cup of yellow cornmeal, fine
- 1 sticks cinnamon
- 1.5 pimento berries
- 0.5 teaspoon of vanilla extract
- 0.25 teaspoon of nutmeg, ground
- 0.25 cup of sweetened condensed milk

Cooking Instructions:

1. Pour 3 cups of water and 1 cup of milk to Instant pot.
2. In a medium bowl, whisk together 1 cup of water and cornmeal until fully combined.
3. Add the mixture to Instant Pot and whisk. Add the cinnamon sticks, pimento berries, vanilla extract, and nutmeg. Close and lock the lid in place.
4. Select the Porridge function for 6 minutes. When the timer beeps, do a natural pressure release for about 10 minutes.
5. Add the sweetened condensed milk to sweeten.
6. Serve and enjoy!

Mac and Cheese

Preparation time: 10 minutes

Cook time: 10 minutes

Total time: 20 minutes

Serves: 2

Ingredients:

- 2 oz. (about 1 cup) macaroni noodles
- ½ cup of vegetable broth
- 1 tbsp. of unsalted butter
- 1/8 tsp. of garlic powder
- 4 oz. of grated extra sharp cheddar
- 1 oz. (1/8 cup) grated Parmesan cheese
- 1 tbsp. of sour cream

Cooking Instructions:

1. Add the macaroni noodles, broth, butter and garlic powder into the bottom of your Instant Pot and give everything a good stir.
2. Close and lock the lid. Select Manual, High Pressure for 5 minutes. When the timer beeps, do a quick pressure release.
3. Carefully remove the lid and add all remaining ingredients like cheddar, Parmesan and sour cream. Give everything a good stir and let to rest for about 5 minutes.
4. The cheese should be melted and the macaroni and cheese mixture should be smooth. Serve immediately and enjoy!

Creamy Grits with Cheddar and Jalapeño

Preparation time: 10 minutes

Cook time: 45 minutes

Total time: 55 minutes

Servings: 2

Calories: 360kcal

Ingredients:

- 1 slices of bacon, chopped
- 0.5 jalapeño peppers, chopped with seeds removed
- 0.25 cup of stone ground grits
- 0.75 cup of water
- 0.25 cup of heavy cream
- 2 ounces of sharp cheddar cheese, shredded
- 0.5 ounces of cream cheese
- Pinch of salt to taste

Cooking Instructions:

1. Place the bacon to insert and select the Sauté button. Cook the bacon on one side for about 8 minutes. Add the bacon pieces until all pieces are cooked.
2. Remove the bacon from heat and pat dry with a paper towel. Drain off any excess bacon grease from Instant Pot, and leave about 2 tablespoons of bacon grease.
3. Add the chopped jalapeño to the pot and stir until softened, about 2 minutes. Add the grits and stir for additional 10 seconds.
4. Pour water and remove any browned bits stuck to the bottom of the pot with a wooden spoon. Stir in heavy cream and salt.
5. Close and lock the lid. Select Manual, High Pressure for 10 minutes. When the timer beeps, do a natural pressure release for about 10 minutes.
6. Carefully remove the lid and stir in cheddar cheese and cream cheese. Let the grits rest for about 5 minutes. Top with pieces of bacon. Serve and enjoy!

Cinnamon Crunch Oatmeal

Preparation time: 2 minutes

Cook time: 2 minutes

Total time: 4 minutes

Servings: 2

Calories: 305kcal

Ingredients:

- 0.5 medium head of cauliflower or 4 cups of riced cauliflower
- 1 cup of almond milk or dairy-free milk
- 3 tablespoons of coconut sugar or ¼ cup of maple syrup
- 1 teaspoon of cinnamon powder
- 0.25 teaspoon of nutmeg
- 0.5 teaspoon of pure vanilla extract
- 1 tablespoon of tapioca starch
- 0.5 cup of toasted nuts and/or seeds
- Extra toppings: sliced fresh fruits, dried fruits, toasted coconut chips, cacao nibs, chocolate chips, nut butter, etc.

Cooking Instructions:

1. If you desired a whole cauliflower head, trim off the leaves and cut off the florets from the roots.
2. Grate the cauliflower with a cheese grater or a food processor into the size of rice. Add the almond milk, coconut sugar, cinnamon, nutmeg, and vanilla extract to the pot.
3. Give everything a good stir. Add the rice cauliflower on top of the liquid. Close and lock the lid. Select Manual, High Pressure for 2 minutes.
4. When the timer beeps, do a quick pressure release. Carefully remove the lid and sprinkle tapioca starch over the oatmeal. Give everything a good stir to thicken.

5. Add more tapioca starch if you desire the texture a bit thicker. Scoop into bowls and top with nut, seeds, and/or your desired toppings.
6. Serve warm or chilled and enjoy!

Instant Pot Spaghetti

Preparation time: 20 minutes

Cook time: 8 minutes

Total time: 28 minutes

Serves: 2

Ingredients:

- 1 tbsp. of olive oil
- ½ pound of lean ground beef (or turkey)
- ½ yellow onion, diced
- 1 clove garlic, minced
- ½ tsp. of dried basil
- ½ tsp. of dried oregano
- ½ tsp. of salt
- Freshly ground black pepper
- 1 cup of jarred spaghetti sauce
- 2 tbsp. of tomato paste
- 1 ¼ cups of chicken broth (or water)
- 2 tbsp. of Parmesan cheese, plus extra for serving
- 6 oz. of spaghetti noodles

Cooking Instructions:

1. Press the Sauté button on your Instant Pot and add the olive oil. Add the ground beef and sauté for about 3 minutes, stirring occasionally.
2. Add the chopped onion. Sauté for about 4 minutes, stirring frequently. Add the garlic, basil, oregano, salt, pepper, spaghetti sauce, tomato paste broth and Parmesan cheese.

3. Give everything a good stir. Press the Cancel function. Break the noodles in half, and add them into the tomato mixture, ensuring they are with the cooking liquid.
4. Close and lock the lid. Select Manual, High Pressure for 8 minutes. When the timer beeps, do a quick pressure release. Carefully remove the lid and stir.
5. If it's still too much liquid for you, press Sauté function and cook for about 2 minutes to reduce the liquid.
6. Serve topped with more Parmesan and enjoy!

Peaches and Cream Oatmeal

Preparation time: 3 minutes

Cook time: 10 minutes

Total time: 13 minutes

Serves: 2

Ingredients:

- 1 cup of rolled oats
- 2 cups of water
- ½ peach, chopped
- ½ tsp. of vanilla
- 1 tbsp. of flax meal
- ¼ cup of chopped almonds
- A splash of milk, cream, or non-dairy milk
- Maple syrup to taste

Cooking Instructions:

1. Add the oats, water, peaches, and vanilla into the bottom of your Instant Pot. Close and lock the lid.
2. Select the Porridge button to cook for 3 minutes. When the timer beeps, do a natural pressure release for about 10 minutes.
3. Carefully open the lid and stir. Divide between 2 bowls, top with your desired ingredients.
4. Serve immediately and enjoy!

Mexican Breakfast Casserole

Preparation time: 5 minutes

Cook time: 15 minutes

Total time: 20 minutes

Servings: 2

Calories: 356kcal

Ingredients:

- 0.5 tbsp. of olive oil
- 0.25 lb. of pork sausage or turkey sausage or chorizo
- 0.25 cup of diced yellow onion
- 0.25 cup of diced red bell pepper
- 1 cloves garlic, minced
- 0.5 large sweet potato (shredded or cubed) about 2 cups
- 3 large eggs
- 0.25 tsp. of chili powder
- A pinch of cayenne pepper
- Sea salt and ground pepper to taste
- 0.5 cup of water
- 0.5 tbsp. of coconut oil, ghee, or butter

Cooking Instructions:

1. Press the Sauté function on your Instant Pot and add the oil. Add the sausage and break it apart with a wooden spatula.
2. Add the onion, sweet potato, and peppers, and sauté for about 3 minutes or until softened. Add the garlic and sauté for additional 1 minute.

3. Pour the potato mixture into a greased 7-cup baking dish, and Press the Cancel function. In a medium bowl, whisk together the eggs, salt, pepper, and chili powder.
4. Pour the egg mixture over the potato/sausage mixture in the baking dish. Place the trivet and pour 1 cup of water into the bottom of your Instant Pot.
5. Place the casserole on top of the trivet. Close and lock the lid. Select Manual, High Pressure for 5 minutes. When the timer beeps, do a natural pressure release.
6. Carefully open the lid and remove the casserole from the Instant Pot. Garnish with Pico de Gallo or Salsa, diced avocado, and chopped cilantro. Slice and serve.
7. Serve immediately and enjoy!

Sweet Potatoes

Preparation time: 5 minutes

Cook time: 15 minutes

Total time: 20 minutes

Servings: 2

Calories: 424 kcal

Ingredients:

- 2 medium sweet potatoes (5 ounces / 140 g each)
- 4 eggs
- 1 avocado
- 1 lemon
- 1 hand full cilantro leaves
- Salt and pepper to taste

Cooking Instructions:

1. Place the metal steamer into the bottom of your Instant pot and pour ½ cup of water. Add the sweet potatoes on steamer.
2. Close and lock the lid. Select Manual, High Pressure for 15 minutes. Heat a pan over medium heat and boil the eggs. Make the poached eggs.
3. When the timer beeps, do a quick pressure release. Carefully remove the lid and transfer the sweet potatoes to a bowl.
4. Cut the sweet potatoes in half, place an egg on each half, salt and pepper, add lemon zest, lemon juice, and cilantro.
5. Serve with half an avocado and enjoy!

POULTRY MEALS

Creamy Mushroom and Chicken Wild Rice Stew

Preparation time: 15 minutes

Cook time: 45 minutes

Total time: 1 hour

Servings: 2

Calories: 419 kcal

Ingredients:

- 2.5 carrots, chopped
- 0.5 medium onion, diced
- 1.5 cloves of garlic, minced
- 0.5 cup of uncooked wild rice
- 5 oz. of fresh mushrooms, sliced
- 2.5 cups of vegetable or chicken broth
- 1-1.5 fresh thyme stalks
- 0.5 lb. of boneless, skinless chicken breasts
- Salt and pepper, to taste

Cooking Instructions:

1. Add all the ingredients into the bottom of your Instant Pot. Close and lock the lid.
2. Select Manual, High Pressure for 45 minutes. When the timer beeps, do a natural pressure release.
3. Carefully open the lid and Transfer the chicken to a cutting board. Shred the chicken and add them back into the Instant Pot.
4. Give everything a good stir to combine. Divide evenly into bowls and serve with some crusty bread!

Chicken and Dumplings

Preparation time: 40 minutes

Cook time: 25 minutes

Total time: 1 hour 5 minutes

Serves: 2

Ingredients:

- 1 ½ tbsp. of unsalted butter
- 2 bone-in, skin-on chicken thighs
- 2 tbsp. of flour
- 1 small carrot, diced
- 1 stalk celery, diced
- 1 small onion, diced
- ½ tsp. of salt
- ¼ tsp. of freshly ground black pepper
- 1 tsp. of minced fresh parsley
- 1 quart of homemade chicken stock

For the dumplings:

- ¾ cup of all-purpose flour
- ¼ cup of fine cornmeal
- 1 tsp. of baking powder
- 2 tsp. of chopped fresh parsley (or dried)
- ½ tsp. of salt
- ¼ tsp. of freshly ground black pepper

- 1 tbsp. of melted butter
- ½ cup of milk

Cooking Instructions:

1. Press the Sauté function on your Instant Pot and add the butter to melt. Add the chicken thighs (skin side down) to the pan.
2. Sauté the chicken thighs until golden brown for about 4 minutes. Turn and cook the other side, too. Remove the chicken from the pot, and transfer to a bowl.
3. Add the flour to the pot, and give everything a good stir to form a paste. Add the carrot, celery, onion, salt, pepper, and parsley.
4. Sauté, stirring occasionally for about 2 minutes. Add the chicken stock and return the chicken back to the Instant Pot. Press the Cancel function.
5. Close and lock the lid. Select Manual, High Pressure for 8 minutes. When the timer beeps, do a natural pressure release.
6. Carefully open the lid and remove the chicken from the pot. In a medium bowl, whisk together the flour, cornmeal, baking powder, parsley, salt and pepper to make the dumplings.
7. In another bowl, whisk together the melted butter and milk. Whisk the dry and wet ingredients together for the dumplings. Don't over-mix.
8. Add a large tablespoon-sized chunks of dumplings into the Instant Pot broth. Close and lock the lid. Select Manual, High Pressure for 2 minutes.
9. When the timer beeps, do a quick pressure release. Shred the chicken with two forks and divide it between two plates. Ladle the dumplings and broth into each bowl. Serve immediately and enjoy!

Chicken Stock

Preparation time: 15 minutes

Cook time: 30 minutes

Total time: 45 minutes

Serves: 2

Ingredients:

- 2 bone-in, skin-on chicken thighs
- 1 medium onion, chopped in half
- 1 large carrot
- 2 stalks celery
- 1 bay leaf
- 2 peppercorns
- 1 tsp. of salt

Cooking Instructions:

1. Place all the ingredients (except salt) into the bottom of your Instant Pot. Pour a little water to cover the ingredients.
2. Close and lock the lid. Select Manual, High Pressure for 30 minutes. When the timer beeps, do a natural pressure release.
3. Carefully open the lid and strain the mixture into a bowl. Discard the solids. Add the salt into the broth and stir until dissolved.
4. Pour the broth into a 1-quart Mason jar container and refrigerate for at least 5 days. Serve and enjoy!

Asian Sesame Chicken

Preparation time: 3 minutes

Cook time: 15 minutes

Total time: 18 minutes

Servings: 2

Calories: 273 kcal

Ingredients:

For Sauce:

- 0.25 cup of water
- 0.25 cup of ketchup
- 0.13 cup of soy sauce
- 1 tbsp. of honey
- 1 tbsp. of sesame oil
- 0.5 tsp. of rice wine vinegar
- 0.5 tsp. of minced ginger

For Chicken:

- 1 chicken breasts, diced

To Thicken Sauce:

- 0.5 tbsp. of cornstarch
- 1.5 tbsp. of water

Cooking Instructions:

1. In a medium bowl, combine together all the ingredients. Add the chicken inside the Instant Pot. Pour sauce over chicken.

2. Give everything a good mix to combine. Close and lock the lid. Select Manual, High Pressure for 5 minutes.
3. When the timer beeps, do a quick pressure release. Carefully open the lid and Press the Sauté function.
4. In a medium bowl, mix together the water and cornstarch. Add mixture to the chicken. Sauté for about for 2 minutes or until sauce thickens.
5. Serve and garnish with green onions and sesame seeds.

Butter Chicken

Preparation time: 30 minutes

Cook time: 20 minutes

Total time: 50 minutes

Serves: 2

Ingredients:

- 2 tbsp. of unsalted butter
- 1 medium yellow onion, diced
- ½ of a red bell pepper, diced
- 2 cloves garlic
- 1-inch of ginger, peeled
- 1 tsp. of garam masala, spice blend
- 1 tsp. of turmeric
- 1 tsp. of smoked paprika
- 1 tsp. of ground cumin
- ½ tsp. of salt
- A pinch of cayenne pepper (optional)
- 14-oz. can of tomato sauce
- 4 boneless, skinless chicken thighs, trimmed of fat and cut into 2" pieces
- 1/3 cup of heavy cream
- 1 tbsp. of cornstarch
- Fresh cilantro, optional for serving
- Cooked basmati rice, optional for serving

Cooking Instructions:

1. Press the Sauté function on your Instant Pot and add the butter to melt.
2. Add the diced onion and bell pepper, and give everything a good stir to coat. Grate the garlic and ginger with a micro plane into pan and stir.
3. Add the garam masala, turmeric, paprika, cumin, and salt and give everything a good stir. Add a pinch of cayenne pepper and stir again.
4. Add the tomato sauce and chopped chicken thighs to the pot and stir. Close and lock the lid in place. Select Manual, High Pressure for 10 minutes.
5. When the timer beeps, do a quick pressure release. Carefully remove the lid. In a medium bowl, whisk together the heavy cream and cornstarch.
6. Stir in the heavy cream and cornstarch mixture. Allow the mixture to cook on the residual heat to thicken.
7. Serve over white rice and with chopped cilantro on top.

Honey Garlic Chicken

Preparation time: 5 minutes

Cook time: 20 minutes

Total time: 25 minutes

Servings: 2

Calories: 360 kcal

Ingredients:

- 1/6 cup of honey
- 2 cloves garlic, minced
- ¼ cup of low sodium soy sauce
- ¼ cup of no salt ketchup
- ¼ tsp. of dried oregano
- 1 tbsp. of chopped fresh parsley
- ½ tbsp. of sesame seed oil
- 2 to 3 bone-in, skinless chicken thighs
- Salt and fresh ground pepper, to taste
- ¼ tbsp. of toasted sesame seeds, for garnish
- Sliced green onions, for garnish

Cooking Instructions:

1. In a medium bowl, combine together the honey, minced garlic, soy sauce, ketchup, oregano and parsley and give everything a good mix to combine.
2. Press the Sauté function on your Instant Pot and add the sesame oil. Generously season the chicken thighs with salt and pepper.
3. Place the chicken thighs in the Instant Pot and cook for about 2 to 3 minutes on each side. Add the prepared honey garlic sauce to the pot.

4. Close and lock the lid. Select the Poultry function to cook for 20 minutes. When the timer beeps, do a quick pressure release.
5. Carefully open the lid and transfer the chicken to a serving bowl. Ladle the sauce over the chicken. Garnish with toasted sesame seeds and green onions.
6. Serve and enjoy!

Creamy Chicken Tortellini Soup

Preparation time: 7 minutes

Cook time: 15 minutes

Total time: 22 minutes

Serves: 2

Calories: 359 kcal

Ingredients:

- ½ tbsp. of butter
- ½ yellow onion, diced
- 1 celery stalks, sliced
- 1 carrots, thinly sliced
- 1 garlic clove, minced
- ½ boneless of skinless chicken breasts, cubed
- ½ tsp. of Italian Seasoning
- ½ tsp. of dried thyme
- Salt and fresh ground pepper to taste
- 2 cups of fat free low sodium chicken broth
- 3 oz. of dried cheese tortellini
- ½ bag 4 oz. of fresh baby spinach
- ½ cup of half & half or heavy cream

Cooking Instructions:

1. Press the Sauté function on your Instant Pot and add the butter to melt. Add the diced onions, celery, carrots, garlic, and chicken.

2. Add the salt and pepper, and cook for about 5 minutes or until chicken is browned and veggies are softened. Stir in chicken broth and tortellini.
3. Close and lock the lid. Select Manual, High Pressure for 5 minutes. When the timer beeps, do a natural pressure release for about 10 minutes.
4. Carefully open the lid and press the Sauté function. Stir in the spinach and half & half. Sauté for about 2 minutes, or until soup is heated through.
5. Serve and enjoy!

Turkey Chili

Preparation time: 10 minutes

Cook time: 45 minutes

Total time: 55 minutes

Servings: 2

Calories: 460kcal

Ingredients:

- 0.67 tablespoon of vegetable oil
- 0.33 yellow onion, chopped
- 0.33 red bell pepper, chopped
- 1.33 garlic cloves, chopped
- 1 tablespoon of chili powder
- 0.33 tablespoon of cumin
- 0.33 teaspoon of dried oregano
- 0.17 teaspoon of ground cinnamon
- 0.17 teaspoon of paprika
- 0.17 teaspoon of salt
- 0.17 teaspoon of black pepper
- 0.08 teaspoon of cayenne pepper
- 0.33 pound of ground turkey
- 0.33 can sweet kernel corn, rinsed and drained
- 0.33 can light red kidney beans, rinsed and drained
- 0.33 can dark red kidney beans, rinsed and drained

- 0.33 cup of chicken broth

- 0.33 can of diced tomato

- 0.67 tablespoon of very fine cornmeal (optional)

Cooking Instructions:

1. Press the Sauté function on your Instant Pot and add the vegetable oil. Add the onion and red bell pepper and for about 3 minutes or until softened.
2. Add the garlic cloves and sauté for additional 1 minute. Add the ground turkey and cook, stirring until meat is no longer pink.
3. Add the chili powder, cumin, oregano, cinnamon, paprika, salt, black pepper, and cayenne pepper. Give everything a good stir.
4. Add the corn, kidney beans, and chicken broth and stir again. Add the can diced tomatoes on top and don't stir. Close and lock the lid.
5. Select Manual, High Pressure for 25 minutes. When the timer beeps, do a natural pressure release for about 10 minutes, then quick release any remaining pressure.
6. Carefully remove the lid and stir. If the chili is too watery, press the Sauté function and cook until your desired consistency is achieved. Add 0.67 tablespoon of cornmeal to thicken.
7. Serve immediately and enjoy!

Chicken and Rice

Preparation time: 10 minutes

Cook time: 20 minutes

Total time: 30 minutes

Servings: 2

Calories: 575kcal

Ingredients:

- 0.5 pound of chicken thighs boneless and skinless
- 0.67 tablespoon of lemon juice
- 1.33 tablespoon of light tasting olive oil, separated
- 0.33 teaspoon of dried oregano
- 0.5 teaspoon of garlic powder
- 0.17 teaspoon of ground coriander
- 0.33 medium onion, chopped
- 1 cloves garlic, chopped
- 0.33 teaspoon of turmeric powder
- 0.17 teaspoon of ground cumin
- 0.5 cups of white rice long grain or Jasmine, rinsed
- 0.67 cup of chicken broth, separated
- Salt and pepper to taste

White Sauce:

- 0.17 cup of mayonnaise
- 0.17 cup of Greek yogurt

- 0.33 tablespoon of sugar
- 0.67 tablespoon of white vinegar
- 0.33 teaspoon of lemon juice
- 0.08 cup of fresh parsley, chopped
- Kosher salt and fresh ground pepper

Cooking Instructions:

1. In a medium bowl, whisk together all the white sauce ingredients and set aside. Combine together the chicken, lemon juice, 1.33 tablespoon of olive oil, oregano, garlic powder, and ground coriander.
2. Press the Sauté function on your Instant Pot and add 1.33 tablespoon of olive oil. Add the chicken pieces and sauté until browned on each side, for about 3 minutes.
3. Remove the chicken pieces and set aside. Add about 0.67 cup of chicken broth to the pot and remove any browned bits stuck to the bottom of the pan.
4. Add the onions and garlic and sauté until the onions have softened. Add the turmeric powder, cumin, and rice and give everything a good stir to coat.
5. Add chicken thighs on top of rice, and ensure that they are covered by the broth. Press the Cancel function. Close and lock the lid in place.
6. Select Manual, High Pressure for 10 minutes. When the timer beeps, do a natural pressure release for about 10 minutes, then quick release any remaining pressure.
7. Carefully remove the lid and adjust the seasoning with salt and pepper. Top with the white sauce.
8. Serve with shredded lettuce and chopped tomatoes. Serve and enjoy!

Salsa Chicken

Preparation time: 25 minutes

Cook time: 10 minutes

Total time: 35 minutes

Serves: 2

Ingredients:

- ½ tbsp. of olive oil
- ½ medium onion, diced
- 1 clove garlic, minced
- 8 oz. of salsa
- ½ cup of Simple Truth Organic Chicken Stock
- ¼ tsp. of cumin
- ½ tsp. of ground coriander
- 1/8 tsp. of salt
- Freshly ground black pepper
- 1 cup of long-grain white rice, rinsed
- 1 boneless, skinless chicken breasts (with rib meat)
- 2 oz. of shredded Tillamook Farmstyle Cut Shredded Mexican Blend Cheese
- Cilantro, optional for serving

Cooking Instructions:

1. Press the Sauté function on your Instant Pot and add the oil. Add the diced onion, and sauté for about 4 minutes or until the onions turns translucent.
2. Add in the garlic and sauté, stirring for about 15 seconds. Press the Cancel function. Add the salsa, chicken stock, cumin, coriander, salt, pepper and rice.

3. Give everything a good stir and place the chicken breasts on top. Close and lock the lid in place. Select Manual, High Pressure for 15 minutes.
4. When the timer beeps, do a natural pressure release for about 10 minutes. Carefully open the lid and fluff the ingredients with a fork.
5. In a medium bowl, pour the rice, chicken and salsa mixture. Add the cheese and give everything a good stir to mix. Shred the chicken and add them into the pot.
6. Serve garnished with cilantro. Refrigerate the leftovers in the fridge for up to 3 days.

Chicken Spaghetti

Preparation time: 10 minutes

Cook time: 6 minutes

Total time: 31 minutes

Servings: 2

Calories: 671kcal

Ingredients:

- 1 tablespoon of butter
- 0.5 pound of chicken breast, cut into 1 inch pieces
- 2.67 ounces of baby Bella mushrooms, sliced
- 0.33 small onion, chopped
- 0.17 cup of red bell pepper, chopped
- 0.67 teaspoon of garlic, minced
- 0.33 teaspoon of seasoned salt
- 0.33 teaspoon of paprika
- 0.17 teaspoon of dry basil
- 0.17 teaspoon of red pepper flakes
- 0.83 cup of chicken broth
- 3.33 ounce of thin spaghetti broken in half
- 0.33 cup of heavy cream
- 0.67 cups of medium cheddar cheese, shredded
- Salt and pepper to taste

Cooking Instructions:

1. Press the Sauté function on your Instant Pot and add the butter to melt. Add the onions, mushrooms, and garlic and stir.
2. Sauté until the onions have softened, for about 5 minutes. Add the red bell pepper, seasoned salt, paprika, basil, red pepper flakes and give everything a good stir.
3. Select the "Cancel" function. Place the chicken breast pieces in layer in the Pressure Cooker and sprinkle with salt and pepper. Pour in chicken broth.
4. Arrange the spaghetti noodles in Instant Pot and ensure that they are covered with the cooking liquid. Close and lock the lid.
5. Select Manual, High Pressure for 6 minutes. When the timer beeps, do a quick pressure release. Carefully remove the lid stir to loosen up noodles.
6. Add the heavy cream and cheese and give everything a good stir. Press the Sauté function and cook for about 3 to 5 minutes, stirring to thicken the sauce.
7. Serve and enjoy!

SOUP MEALS

Jalapeño Lime Chicken Soup

Preparation time: 15 minutes

Cook time: 30 minutes

Total time: 45 minutes

Serves: 2

Ingredients:

- 0.5 medium onion, diced
- 1.5 cloves garlic, minced
- 0.5: 2 oz. of can diced green chilies
- Juice of 1 lime
- 0.5 jalapeño, diced
- 0.25 tsp. of ground cumin
- 0.25 tsp. of ground coriander
- 0.5 cup of frozen corn kernels
- 1.5 cups of low-sodium chicken broth
- 0.5: 7.5 oz. can of hominy, drained
- 1 cup of shredded rotisserie chicken
- Salt and pepper, to taste

Cooking Instructions:

1. Add all the ingredients except for the hominy and chicken into the bottom of your Instant Pot. Close and lock the lid.
2. Select the Soup function to cook for 30 minutes. When the timer beeps, do a quick pressure release.

3. Carefully open the lid and add in the hominy and rotisserie chicken to the pot. Close and lock the lid in place.
4. Cook the ingredients for about 10 minutes in the residual heat to warm up the hominy and chicken. Season with more salt and pepper, to taste.
5. Serve and enjoy!

Minestrone Soup

Preparation time: 15 minutes

Cook time: 30 minutes

Total time: 45 minutes

Serves: 2

Ingredients:

- 1.67 stalks celery hearts, sliced
- 1.67 carrots, peeled and sliced
- 0.17 medium onion, diced
- 1 cup of vegetable stock
- 0.33 cup of marinara sauce
- 0.67 tsp. of smoked paprika
- 0.33 tbsp. of Italian seasoning
- Salt and pepper, to taste
- 1 bay leaves
- 0.25 cup of pastina
- 0.33: 5 oz. can of cannellini beans, drained and rinsed

Cooking Instructions:

1. Add all the ingredients into the bottom of your Instant Pot except for the pastina and cannellini beans.
2. Close and lock the lid. Select the Soup function to cook for 30 minutes. When the timer beeps, do a quick pressure release.
3. Carefully open the lid and add in the pastina and beans into the soup. Close and lock the lid.
4. Allow the ingredients to cook for about 10 minutes in the residual heat cook to warm up the beans. Serve and enjoy!

Harvest Butternut Squash Soup

Preparation time: 15 minutes

Cook time: 25 minutes

Total time: 40 minutes

Servings: 2

Calories: 173 kcal

Ingredients:

- 1.25 cup of cubed butternut squash
- 0.5 cup of apple juice (not concentrate)
- 0.25 cup of vegetable stock
- 0.25 cup of pumpkin puree
- 0.38 tsp. of curry powder
- 1 oz. of plain cream cheese
- Salt and pepper, to taste

Cooking Instructions:

1. Add the butternut squash, apple juice, and vegetable stock into the bottom of your Instant Pot. Close and lock the lid.
2. Select Manual, High Pressure for 25 minutes. When the timer beeps, do a quick pressure release.
3. Carefully open the lid and blend the ingredients until smooth with an immersion blender. Add in the pumpkin, curry powder, cream cheese, salt, and pepper.
4. Blend again until smooth. Divide into two plates and serve immediately.

Sausage and Herbed White Bean Soup

Preparation time: 15 minutes

Cook time: 40 minutes

Total time: 55 minutes

Servings: 2

Calories: 355 kcal

Ingredients:

- 4 oz. of cooked Italian chicken sausage, sliced into rounds
- 3 stalks celery, chopped
- 2.5 carrots, chopped
- 0.5 medium onion, chopped
- 1 tbsp. of tomato paste
- 2 sprigs of fresh thyme
- 1 sprigs of fresh rosemary
- 0.5 lb. of dry white beans
- 2.5 cups of chicken stock
- Salt and pepper to taste

Cooking Instructions:

1. Select the Sauté function on your Instant Pot and add 1 tbsp. of vegetables oil. Add the sausage and cook to brown on both sides.
2. Press the Cancel function and add the remaining ingredients. Give everything a good mix. Close and lock the lid.
3. Select Manual, High Pressure for 40 minutes. When the timer beeps, do a quick pressure release.
4. Carefully open the lid and give everything a good stir. Divide into bowls and serve with crusty bread!

Mexican Tortilla Soup

Preparation time: 10 minutes

Cook time: 7 minutes

Total time: 17 minutes

Servings: 2

Calories: 217 kcal

Ingredients:

- ½ lb. of boneless skinless chicken breasts (uncooked/raw)
- ½ can of whole peeled tomatoes, undrained OR ½ can fire-roasted diced tomatoes
- ½ can (5 oz.) red enchilada sauce
- ½ tsp. of minced garlic
- ½ yellow onion, diced
- ½ can (2 oz.) fire-roasted diced green chiles
- ½ can of black beans, drained and rinsed
- ½ can of fire-roasted corn, undrained
- ½ container (16 oz.) chicken stock or broth
- ½ tsp. of ground cumin
- 1 tsp. of chili powder
- ¾ tsp. of paprika
- 1 bay leaf
- Seasoned salt and freshly cracked pepper, to taste
- ½ tbsp. of chopped cilantro

- Tortilla strips, Freshly squeezed lime juice, freshly grated sharp cheddar cheese, ripe avocados, fresh cilantro, optional for serving

Cooking Instructions:

1. Select the Sauté function and add 1 tbsp. of olive oil. Add the minced garlic and diced onion and cook for about 3-4 minutes until the onion begins to soften.
2. Drain the fat from the chicken breasts and add to the Instant Pot along with all the remaining ingredients. Give everything a good stir.
3. Close and lock the lid. Select Manual, High Pressure for 7 minutes. When the timer beeps, do a natural pressure release for about 10 minutes, then quick release any remaining pressure.
4. Carefully open the lid and transfer the chicken to a cutting board. Shred the chicken with two forks and return back to the pot.
5. Adjust the seasoning to taste with salt and pepper and fresh lime if desired. Discard the bay leaf. Divide the soup in bowls.
6. Serve with your desired toppings: freshly grated cheese, sour cream, additional cilantro, fresh lime, and lots of tortilla strips!

Curried Coconut Lentil Soup

Preparation time: 10 minutes

Cook time: 15 minutes

Total time: 25 minutes

Servings: 2

Calories: 310 kcal

Ingredients:

- 0.5 small onion, diced
- 1 garlic cloves, minced
- 0.5 tbsp. of ginger paste
- 0.5 tbsp. of curry powder
- 0.13 tsp. of crushed red pepper flakes
- 0.38 cup of dried red split lentils
- 7.25 oz. can of unsweetened full fat coconut milk
- 0.63 - 0.75 cup of water
- Salt and pepper, to taste
- 7.75 oz. can of crushed tomatoes

Cooking Instructions:

1. Select the Sauté function on your Instant Pot and add the onion, garlic, ginger paste, curry powder, and crushed red pepper flakes.
2. Add the lentils, coconut milk, water, salt, and pepper. Give everything a good mix and bring it to a simmer. Press the Cancel function.
3. Add the can of crushed tomatoes on top and don't stir. Close and lock the lid. Select Manual, High Pressure for 15 minutes.
4. When the timer beeps, do a quick pressure release. Carefully remove the lid and stir. Divide the soup into bowls and garnish with parsley or cilantro on top.
5. Serve immediately and enjoy!

Moroccan Spiced Soup

Preparation time: 15 minutes

Cook time: 20 minutes

Total time: 1 hour

Servings: 2

Calories: 283kcal

Ingredients:

- 0.67 tablespoon of vegetable oil
- 0.33 pound of lamb, cut into 1-inch chunks
- 0.33 onion, sliced
- 0.33 tablespoon of minced garlic
- 0.67 teaspoon of ground cumin
- 0.67 teaspoon of paprika
- 0.5 teaspoon of ground ginger
- 0.33 teaspoon of cinnamon
- 0.08 teaspoon of allspice
- 1 cup of chicken broth
- 0.33 (7.75 ounce) can chickpeas, drained and rinsed
- 0.33 (7.75 ounce) can diced tomatoes
- 2.67 ounces of spinach
- Salt and pepper to taste

Cooking Instructions:

1. Select the Sauté function on your Instant Pot and add the vegetable oil. Add the lamb meat and sauté for about 4 minutes or until browned.
2. Add the onion and garlic and cook, stirring occasionally until the onion has softened, for about 3 minutes.
3. Add the cumin, paprika, ginger, cinnamon, allspice and stir for additional 1 minute. Add the chicken broth and scrape any browned bits stuck to the bottom of the pot.
4. Add the chickpeas and diced tomatoes and don't stir. Close and lock the lid. Select Manual, High Pressure for 20 minutes.
5. When the timer beeps, do a natural pressure release for about 10 minutes, then quick release any remaining pressure.
6. Carefully remove the lid and stir in spinach. Adjust the seasoning with salt and pepper to taste. Divide the soup into bowls.
7. Serve immediately and enjoy!

Lentil Soup with Sausage

Preparation time: 10 minutes

Cook time: 15 minutes

Total time: 25 minutes

Servings: 2

Calories: 276kcal

Ingredients:

- 0.25 pound of Italian sausage ground
- 0.25 medium onion, chopped
- 0.25 stalk celery, chopped
- 0.25 medium carrot, chopped
- 0.25 medium zucchini, chopped
- 0.75 garlic cloves, minced
- 1 cup of chicken broth
- 0.25 cup of brown or green lentils
- 0.5 teaspoon of dried basil
- 0.25 teaspoon of dried oregano
- 0.5 14 ½ cans of diced tomatoes undrained
- 0.06 cup of fresh parsley
- Sour cream, optional
- Parmesan cheese, optional

Cooking Instructions:

1. Press the Sauté function on your Instant Pot and add the Italian sausage. Sauté the sausage until brown, breaking up the meat in the process.
2. Add the onion, celery, carrot, zucchini, and garlic cloves and cook, stirring occasionally until vegetables soften for about 3 minutes. Select the "Cancel" function.
3. Add the chicken broth, lentils, dried basil, and oregano into the bottom of your Instant Pot and give everything a good stir.
4. Pour diced tomatoes on top of the mixture. Close and lock the lid. Select Manual, High Pressure for 15 minutes. When the timer beeps, do a natural pressure release.
5. Carefully remove the lid and add fresh parsley and stir. Season with salt and pepper to taste. Top with sour cream or parmesan cheese. Serve and enjoy!

SEA FOOD MEALS

Shrimp Paella

Preparation time: 10 minutes

Cook time: 5 minutes

Total time: 15 minutes

Servings: 2

Calories: 318kcal

Ingredients:

- 0.5 pound of jumbo shrimp, shell and tail on frozen
- 0.5 cup of Jasmine rice
- 2 tablespoons of butter
- 0.5 onion, chopped
- 2 cloves garlic, chopped
- 0.5 red pepper, chopped
- 0.5 cup of chicken broth
- 0.25 cup of white wine
- 0.5 teaspoon of paprika
- 0.5 teaspoon of turmeric
- 0.25 teaspoon of salt
- 0.13 teaspoon of black pepper
- 0.5 pinch saffron threads
- 0.13 teaspoon of red pepper flakes

- 0.13 cup of cilantro, optional

Cooking Instructions:

1. Press the Sauté function on your Instant Pot and add the butter to melt. Add the onions and sauté until softened.
2. Add the garlic and sauté for additional 1 minute. Add the paprika, turmeric, salt, black pepper, red pepper flakes, and saffron threads.
3. Give everything a good stir and cook for about 1 minute. Add the red peppers, rice and stir. Sauté for another 1 minute.
4. Add the chicken broth and white wine and remove any browned bits stuck to the bottom of the pot. Place the shrimp on top.
5. Press the Cancel function. Close and lock the lid. Select Manual, High Pressure for 5 minutes. When the timer beeps, do a quick pressure release.
6. Carefully open the lid and remove shrimp from pot and peel if desired. Serve with cilantro and enjoy!

Cajun Dirty Rice

Preparation time: 10 minutes

Cook time: 6 minutes

Total time: 16 minutes

Servings: 2

Calories: 525kcal

Ingredients:

- 0.33 pound of pork sausage
- 0.17 pound of chicken livers, finely chopped
- 0.33 medium onion, chopped
- 0.67 stalks celery, chopped
- 0.17 green bell pepper, chopped
- 0.33 tablespoon of minced garlic
- 0.33 tablespoon of Creole seasoning
- 0.33 teaspoon of dried thyme
- 0.33 tablespoon of Worcestershire sauce
- 0.33 tablespoon of hot sauce
- 0.67 cup of white rice, rinsed
- 0.42 cup of beef broth
- 0.33 cup of water
- 0.33 bay leaf
- 0.08 cup of fresh parsley, chopped

Cooking Instructions:

1. Press the Sauté function on your Instant Pot and add the pork sausage.
2. Cook, stirring to break up the meat pieces. Add the chicken livers. Sauté, stirring until the meat has browned on both sides.
3. Add the onion, celery, green bell pepper, minced garlic, Creole seasoning, dried thyme, Worcestershire sauce, and hot sauce.
4. Cook, stirring until onions and bell peppers have softened for about 2 minutes. Add rice, beef broth, and water and stir to remove any browned bits stuck to the pot.
5. Add the bay leaf on top of mixture. Select the Cancel function. Close and lock the lid. Select Manual, High Pressure for 6 minutes.
6. When the timer beeps, do a natural pressure release for about 10 minutes. Carefully open the lid and discard the bay leaf.
7. Add fresh parsley to rice. Fluff with fork before serving. Serve immediately and enjoy!

Salmon with Creamy Herb Parmesan Sauce

Preparation time: 5 minutes

Cook time: 15 minutes

Total time: 20 minutes

Servings: 2

Calories: 655.7kcal

Ingredients:

- 2 frozen salmon filets
- 0.25 cup of water
- 0.75 teaspoon of minced garlic
- 0.25 cup of heavy cream
- 0.5 cup of parmesan cheese, grated
- 0.5 tablespoon of chopped fresh chives
- 0.5 tablespoon of chopped fresh parsley
- 0.5 tablespoon of fresh dill
- 0.5 teaspoon of fresh lemon juice
- Salt and pepper to taste

Cooking Instructions:

1. Pour water and garlic into the bottom of your Instant Pot. Add the salmon on top of trivet. Close and lock the lid in place.
2. Select Manual, High Pressure for 5 minutes. When the timer beeps, do a quick pressure release. Press the Cancel function.
3. Carefully open the lid and remove salmon. Press the Sauté function. Once water starts to boil, whisk in the heavy cream and bring to a simmer.
4. Let it to boil for about 2 minutes. Press the Cancel function and remove insert from heat. Whisk in chives, parsley, dill, parmesan cheese, and lemon juice.
5. Adjust the seasoning with salt and pepper to taste. Serve and enjoy!

Sweet and Spicy Pineapple Shrimp

Preparation time: 10 minutes

Cook time: 2 minutes

Total time: 12 minutes

Servings: 2

Ingredients:

- 0.5 large red bell pepper, sliced
- 6 oz. Calrose rice or quinoa
- 0.38 cup of unsweetened pineapple juice
- 0.13 cup of dry white wine
- 0.13 cup of fresh water
- 1 tbsp. of soy sauce
- 1 tbsp. of Thai sweet chili sauce
- 0.5 tbsp. of sambal Oelek ground chili paste
- 0.5 lb. of large shrimp frozen w/ tails
- 2 scallions chopped, white and greens separated
- 0.75 cup of pineapple chunks, drained

Cooking Instructions:

1. Squeeze out the juice from Pineapple and set the pineapple chunks aside. Set aside ¾ cup of pineapple juice.
2. Add the red bell peppers, pineapple juice, wine, water, chili sauce, soy sauce, sambal Oelek, and rice and white part of chopped scallions into the Instant Pot.
3. Add the frozen shrimp on top. Close and lock the lid in place. Select Manual, High Pressure for 2 minutes.
4. When the timer beeps, do a natural pressure release for about 10 minutes. Carefully open the lid and add the pineapple chunks and scallion greens and mix.
5. Serve immediately and enjoy!

Creamy Shrimp Scampi

Preparation time: 5 minutes

Cook time: 10 minutes

Total time: 15 minutes

Servings: 2

Calories: 312 kcal

Ingredients:

- 0.67 tbsp. of butter
- 0.33 lb. of shrimp, frozen
- 1.33 cloves garlic, minced
- 0.08-0.17 tsp. of red pepper flakes
- 0.17 tsp. of paprika
- 0.67 cup of Carbanada low carb pasta (uncooked)
- 0.33 cup of water or chicken broth
- 0.17 cup of half and half
- 0.17 cup of parmesan cheese
- Salt and pepper to taste

Cooking Instructions:

1. Press the Sauté function on your Instant Pot and add the butter to melt. Add in garlic and red pepper flakes.
2. Sauté until the garlic has browned for about 2 minutes. Add the paprika and then the frozen shrimp, salt, pepper, and noodles.
3. Pour in the broth. Close and lock the lid in place. Select Manual, High Pressure for about 2 minutes.
4. When the timer beeps, do a quick pressure release. Carefully remove the lid and press the Sauté function.

5. Add in half and half and cheese, and give everything a good stir until melted. Serve immediately and enjoy!

Shrimp Risotto

Preparation time: 5 minutes

Cook time: 10 minutes

Total time: 15 minutes

Servings: 2

Calories: 244 kcal

Ingredients:

- 0.33 cup of jasmine rice
- 0.33 cup of water
- 0.67 tbsp. of butter
- 0.33 tbsp. of lemon juice
- 0.08 cup of frozen vegetables
- 0.33 lb. of frozen raw shrimp
- 0.08 cup of shredded Parmesan cheese
- Salt and pepper to taste

Cooking Instructions:

1. Press the Sauté function on your Instant Pot and add the butter to melt. Add the rice, water, lemon juice, salt and pepper.
2. Add the frozen shrimp and frozen vegetables on top. Close and lock the lid in place. Select Manual, High Pressure for 5 minutes.
3. When the timer beeps, do a quick pressure release. Carefully remove the lid and allow the rice to absorb the water.
4. Serve with Parmesan cheese and enjoy!

Crustless Crab Quiche

Preparation time: 10 minutes

Cook time: 50 minutes

Total time: 1 hour

Servings: 2

Calories: 395 kcal

Ingredients:

- 2 eggs, beaten
- 0.5 cup of half and half
- 0.25 -0.5 teaspoon of salt
- 0.5 tsp. of pepper
- 0.5 tsp. of sweet smoked paprika
- 0.5 tsp. of Simply Organic Herbes de Provence, 1 ounce of zHerbes de Provence
- 0.5 cup of shredded parmesan or Swiss cheese
- 0.5 cup of chopped green onions, green and white parts
- 4 ounces imitation crab meat about 2 cups OR 4 ounces of real crab meat, or a mix of crab and chopped raw shrimp

Cooking Instructions:

1. In a medium bowl, beat together eggs and half-and-half. Add salt, pepper, sweet smoked paprika, Herbes de Provence, and shredded cheese.
2. Give everything a good stir with a fork. Stir in chopped green onions. Add in your desired imitation crab meat or the real crab meat or mix of crab meat and chopped raw shrimp.
3. Lay out a sheet of aluminum foil and place the spring form pan on top of the sheet. Pour in the egg mixture into your spring form pan.
4. Loosely cover the pan with foil. Pour 2 cups of water into the bottom of your Instant Pot and place the steamer rack.

5. Place the covered spring form pan on the trivet. Close and lock the lid in place. Select Manual, High Pressure for 40 minutes.
6. When the timer beeps, do a natural pressure release for about 10 minutes, then quick release any remaining pressure.
7. Carefully open the lid and remove the hot silicone pan. Loosen the edges of the quiche from the pan with a knife. Flip onto a serving bowl.
8. Serve hot or at room temperature and enjoy!

Shrimp Coconut Curry

Preparation time: 10 minutes

Cook time: 10 minutes

Total time: 20 minutes

Servings: 2

Calories: 192 kcal

Ingredients:

- 0.5 lb. of shrimp shelled, deveined
- 0.5 tbsp. of minced ginger, minced
- 0.5 tablespoon garlic minced
- 0.25 tsp. of turmeric
- 0.5 tsp. of salt
- 0.25 tsp. of cayenne pepper
- 0.5 tsp. of garam masala
- 0.25 can of unsweetened coconut milk

Cooking Instructions:

1. In a medium bowl, mix together all of the ingredients. Cover the foil with a piece of aluminum foil.
2. Pour 1 cup of water into the bottom of your Instant Pot and place the trivet. Add the shrimp and coconut mixture on top the trivet.
3. Close and lock the lid in place. Select Manual, High Pressure for 4 minutes. When the timer beeps, do a quick pressure release.
4. Carefully open the lid and give everything a good mix. Add a little extra coconut milk if desired.
5. Serve immediately and enjoy!

Shrimp Scampi Paella

Preparation time: 10 minutes

Cook time: 5 minutes

Total time: 15 minutes

Servings: 2

Ingredients:

- 0.5 lb. of frozen wild caught shrimp, 16-20 count shell & tail on
- 0.5 cup of Jasmine Rice
- 0.13 cup of organic grass-fed butter or ghee
- 0.13 cup of fresh parsley, chopped
- 0.5 tsp. of sea salt
- 0.13 tsp. of black pepper
- 0.5 pinch of crushed red pepper flakes
- 0.5 medium lemon, juiced
- 0.5 pinch of saffron
- 0.75 cup of water or chicken broth
- 2 cloves garlic, minced
- Organic grass-fed butter or ghee, optional for garnish
- Grated hard cheese parmesan, romano or asiago optional for garnish
- Fresh parsley, chopped, optional for garnish
- Lemon, juiced, optional for garnish

Cooking Instructions:

1. Add all the ingredients into the bottom of your Instant Pot, and place the frozen shell-on-shrimp on the top.
2. Close and lock the lid in place and ensure that the valve is in sealing position. Select Manual, High Pressure for 5 minutes.
3. When the timer beeps, do a quick pressure release. Carefully remove the lid. The paella can be served with the shells on the shrimp or peeled, if desired.
4. Return the peeled shrimp back into the rice and discard the shells.
5. Serve with a garnish of fresh parsley, butter, grated cheese and squeeze of lemon juice if desired.

Salmon with Chili-Lime Sauce

Preparation time: 10 minutes

Cook time: 5 minutes

Total time: 15 minutes

Servings: 2

Calories: 400 kcal

Ingredients:

For Steaming Salmon:

- 2 salmon fillets, about 5 oz. each
- 1 cup of water
- Sea salt to taste
- Freshly ground black pepper to taste

For Chili-Lime Sauce:

- 1 jalapeno, seeds removed and diced
- 1 lime, juiced
- 2 cloves garlic, minced
- 1 tbsp. of honey
- 1 tbsp. of olive oil
- 1 tbsp. of hot water
- 1 tbsp. of chopped fresh parsley
- ½ tsp. of paprika
- ½ tsp. of cumin

Cooking Instructions:

1. In a medium bowl, combine together all of the sauce ingredients and give everything a good mix. Set the mixture aside.
2. Pour the 1 cup of water into the bottom of your Instant Pot and place the steam rack. Add the salmon fillets on top of the steam rack.
3. Generously season the top of the salmon fillets with salt and pepper. Close and lock the lid in place. Select the Steam function to cook for 5 minutes.
4. When the timer beeps, do a quick pressure release. Carefully remove the lid and transfer the salmon to a serving bowl.
5. Drizzle with chili-lime sauce and serve.

Salmon, Broccoli & Potatoes

Preparation time: 1 minute

Cook time: 4 minutes

Total time: 5 minutes

Servings: 2

Ingredients:

- 144 g of salmon fillet
- 140 g of broccoli, chopped into florets
- 500 g of new potatoes
- 2 teaspoon of butter
- 160 ml of water
- Salt and pepper to taste
- Fresh herbs, optional

Cooking Instructions:

1. Pour 160ml of water into the bottom of your Instant Pot and place the steamer rack. Generously season the potatoes with salt, pepper and fresh herbs.
2. Generously season the salmon and broccoli with salt and pepper. Add the potatoes onto the steaming rack and smother them with the butter.
3. Close and lock the lid in place. Select the Steam function to cook for 2 minutes. When the timer beeps, do a quick pressure release.
4. Carefully remove the lid. Add the broccoli florets and salmon onto the rack and cook for additional 2 minutes.
5. When the timer beeps, do a quick pressure release. Carefully remove the lid and allow to cool from Keep Warm function.
6. Serve and enjoy!

Lemon Pepper Salmon

Preparation time: 5 minutes

Cook time: 10 minutes

Total time: 15 minutes

Servings: 2

Calories: 296 kcal

Ingredients:

- 0.5 cup of water
- A few sprigs of parsley dill, tarragon, basil or a combo
- 0.67 lb. of salmon filet skin on
- 2 tsp. of ghee, divided
- 0.17 tsp. of salt
- 0.33 tsp. of pepper
- 0.33 lemon, thinly sliced
- 0.67 zucchini, julienned
- 0.67 red bell pepper, julienned
- 0.67 carrot, julienned

Cooking Instructions:

1. Pour the water and herbs into the bottom of your Instant Pot and place the steamer rack. Add the salmon, skin down on rack.
2. Drizzle salmon with ghee, season with salt and pepper, and cover with lemon slices. Close and lock the lid in place.
3. Select the Steam function to cook for about 3 minutes. Meanwhile, julienne your veggies. When the timer beeps, do a quick pressure release.
4. Carefully remove the lid and remove rack with salmon onto a bowl. Remove herbs and discard.

5. Add the veggies and secure the lid in place. Press the "Sauté" function and cook the veggies for about 2 minutes.
6. Serve with salmon and add remaining teaspoon of ghee to the pot and pour some sauce over them if desired.

BEEF MEALS

Beef and Broccoli

Preparation time: 15 minutes

Cook time: 25 minutes

Total time: 40 minutes

Servings: 2

Calories: 343 kcal

Ingredients:

- 1 lb. of boneless beef chuck roast cubed into 2" cubes
- 1 cup of beef broth
- ½ cup of low-sodium soy sauce
- 1/3 cup of dark brown sugar
- 1 tbsp. of sesame oil
- 3 cloves garlic, minced
- 2-3 cups of fresh broccoli florets, blanched
- 2 tbsp. of cornstarch
- 3 tbsp. of water

Cooking Instructions:

1. Add the cubed beef into the bottom of your Instant Pot. In a medium bowl, whisk together the beef broth, soy sauce, dark brown sugar, sesame oil, and minced garlic.
2. Pour over the beef into the pot. Close and lock the lid in place. Select Manual, High Pressure for 24 minutes. Meanwhile, blanch your broccoli.
3. In a separate bowl, whisk together the cornstarch and water and ensuring that the cornstarch is completely dissolved.

4. When the timer beeps, do a natural pressure release for about 20 minutes, then quick release any remaining pressure.
5. Carefully remove the lid and press the Sauté function. Once the liquid begins to bubble, add the cornstarch slurry and the broccoli.
6. Cook for a couple of minutes to thicken the sauce. Give everything a good mix. Serve over white rice and enjoy!

Beef Tips and Gravy with Mashed Potatoes

Serves: 2

Preparation time: 5 minutes

Cook time: 15 minutes

Total time: 20 minutes

Ingredients:

- ½ tablespoon of olive oil
- ½ chopped onion
- ½ lb. sirloin steak, cubed
- 0.75 cup of red wine
- ½ cup of beef broth
- 8 ounces of whole baby mushrooms
- 2 large potatoes, cubed
- 1 tablespoon of corn starch
- ½ tablespoon of gravy master

For mashed Potatoes:

- 1 tablespoon of butter
- ½ cup of milk
- Salt and pepper

Cooking Instructions:

1. Press the Sauté function on your Instant Pot and add the olive oil. Add the onion, steak and cook, until browned for about 2 minutes.
2. Add the wine, broth and mushrooms. Place the steamer rack on top of mixture and add potatoes. Close and lock the lid in place.

3. Select Manual, High Pressure for 15 minutes. When the timer beeps, do a quick pressure release. Carefully remove the lid and remove the potatoes.
4. Mash the potatoes with butter and milk till creamy and smooth. In a medium bowl, mix together the 1 tablespoon of corn starch and broth.
5. Press the Sauté function. Pour the mixture along with the gravy master into the pot and mix. Give everything a good stir to thicken.
6. Serve and enjoy!

Cubed Steak and Gravy

Serves: 2

Preparation time: 10 minutes

Cook time: 4 minutes

Total time: 14 minutes

Ingredients:

- 1 lb. of cube steak
- 1 5 ounces can French onion soup
- ½ packet of Au Jus Gravy Mix
- 5 ounce of water
- ½ tablespoon of steak sauce, optional
- 1 tablespoon of corn starch

Cooking Instructions:

1. Add the steak into the bottom of your Instant Pot and pour over gravy mix. Add the can of onion soup. Pour in water with the same can.
2. Close and lock the lid in place and ensure that the valve is in sealing position. Select Manual, High Pressure for 4 minutes.
3. When the timer beeps, do a natural pressure release for about 5 minutes, then quick release any remaining pressure.
4. Carefully remove the lid. Press the Sauté function and bring the pot to a boil. Whisk in cornstarch if your gravy is not thick enough.
5. Serve and enjoy!

Beef Stroganoff

Preparation time: 20 minutes

Cook time: 3 minutes

Total time: 23 minutes

Servings: 2

Calories: 705kcal

Ingredients:

- 10 oz. of beef sirloin steak, sliced into 2 inch chunks
- 5 oz. of cremini or wild mushrooms, sliced
- 2.67 oz. of yellow onion, sliced
- 1 cloves fresh garlic, minced
- 0.67 tsp. of extra virgin olive oil
- 1 tbsp. of butter
- 0.67 tsp. of kosher salt
- 0.25 tsp. of Hungarian paprika
- 0.25 tsp. of freshly ground black pepper
- 2 tbsp. of potato starch
- 1.33 oz. of dry sherry wine
- 3.33 oz. of beef broth unsalted
- 0.5 tbsp. of Worcestershire sauce
- 0.5 tbsp. of Dijon mustard
- 2.67 oz. of sour cream
- 5 oz. of wide egg noodles, prepared according to package directions

- Fresh flat leaf parsley, for garnish

Cooking Instructions:

1. Slice the beef sirloin and season with salt, pepper and paprika. Add the potato starch and give everything a good mix.
2. Press the Sauté function on your Instant Pot and add the olive oil and half of the butter to melt. Add the beef and cook until brown for about 1 minute.
3. Remove Beef to a bowl. Remove any browned bits stuck to the bottom of the pot with half the Sherry. Add the rest of the butter, onions and mushrooms.
4. Cook for about 6 minutes. Add the garlic and cook for 30 seconds. Add the remaining sherry and mix in Worcestershire sauce, Dijon mustard and broth.
5. Add the beef back into the pot. Close and lock the lid in place. Select Manual, High Pressure for 3 minutes. When the timer beeps, do a quick pressure release.
6. Press the Sauté function and cook for about 5 minutes to reduce the liquid. Adjust the seasoning with salt and pepper, if desired.
7. Add the sour cream into a large measuring cup and pour ½ cup of hot liquid to temper and give the mixture a good whisk. Slowly pour the sour cream into the cooking pot and whisk.
8. Serve over egg noodles or rice, with a garnish of parsley. Serve immediately and enjoy!

Chili Lime Short Ribs

Preparation time: 10 minutes

Cook time: 40 minutes

Total time: 45 minutes

Servings: 2

Ingredients:

- 1.5-2 pound of beef short ribs, sliced into sections
- 0.5 tablespoon of chili powder
- 0.5 tablespoon of cumin
- 0.5 teaspoon of onion powder
- 0.5 teaspoon of dried oregano
- 0.75 teaspoon of sea salt
- 0.25 teaspoon of ground black pepper
- 0.25 teaspoon of coriander
- 0.13 teaspoon of cayenne, optional
- 2 garlic cloves, minced
- Juice and zest of 2 limes, plus more for garnish
- 1 tablespoon of coconut oil
- 0.17 cup of apple cider vinegar
- Chopped cilantro, for garnish

Cooking Instructions:

1. In a medium bowl, combine together the chili powder, cumin, onion powder, oregano, sea salt, black pepper, coriander, cayenne, garlic cloves, and lime zest.

2. Give everything a good mix. Sprinkle the short ribs with spices until they are evenly covered. Press the Sauté function on your Instant Pot and add the coconut oil.
3. Add the short ribs to the Instant Pot and cook for about 5 minutes to brown on both sides. Press the Cancel function. Pour in lime juice and apple cider vinegar.
4. Close and lock the lid in place. Select the Stew function to cook for 35 minutes. When the timer beeps, do a natural pressure release for about 10 minutes.
5. Carefully remove the lid and give everything a good stir. Sprinkle with cilantro and more lime juice. Serve immediately and enjoy!

Sloppy Joes

Preparation time: 25 minutes

Cook time: 3 minutes

Total time: 28 minutes

Servings: 2

Ingredients:

- 0.5 tbsp. of extra virgin olive oil
- 0.38 lb. of lean ground beef
- 0.31 cups/200g of sweet onion, diced
- 0.31 cups/200g of green bell pepper, diced
- 0.5 cloves fresh garlic, minced
- 0.06 cup of red wine vinegar
- 0.63 tbsp. of Worcestershire sauce
- 0.88 tbsp. of dark brown sugar
- 0.38 cups/12 ounce of tomato puree
- 0.5 tbsp. of tomato paste
- 0.5 tsp. of sea salt
- 0.13 tsp. of freshly ground black pepper
- 0.25 tsp. of chili powder
- 0.13 tsp. of gravy/ground mustard seed
- 0.03-0.06 tsp. of crushed red pepper flakes
- 2 good quality hamburger buns

Cooking Instructions:

1. Press the Sauté function on your Instant Pot and add the oil. Add the onions, peppers, garlic and ground beef.
2. Cook the ingredients until ground beef is slightly brown. Drain some of the grease. And leave about ¼ cup of liquid.
3. Pour in red wine vinegar and remove any browned bits stuck to the bottom of the pot. Mix in Worcestershire sauce, brown sugar and tomato puree.
4. Add salt, pepper, chili, mustard, red pepper flakes and tomato paste and give everything a good mix. Close and lock the lid in place.
5. Select Manual, High Pressure for 3 minutes. When the timer beeps, do a natural pressure release for about 15 minutes.
6. Carefully remove the lid and press the Sauté function. Bring the pot to a boil until the sauce has thickened.
7. Serve on toasted and buttered Kaiser Rolls or hamburger buns. Serve and enjoy!

Beef Vindaloo

Servings: 2

Preparation time: 1 day

Cook time: 55 minutes

Total time: 1 day 55 minutes

Ingredients:

- 500 g of beef shin, cut into 3cm chunks
- 100 g of onion, cut into wedges
- 2 green Chile, sliced
- 2 tomatoes, chopped
- 150 ml of water
- 2 tablespoons of ghee

For the Marinade:

- ½ teaspoon of ground cinnamon
- ¼ teaspoon of ground cloves
- 1 teaspoon of Armchoor, AKA mango powder
- 1 teaspoon of ground turmeric
- ½ teaspoon of ground cumin
- 2 tablespoons of Kashmiri chili powder
- ½ teaspoon of ground black pepper
- 50 g of onion
- 8 cloves garlic
- 25 g of ginger

- 1 tablespoon of lemon juice
- 1 teaspoon of coarse sea salt
- 1 teaspoon of honey
- 50 ml of tamarind pulp
- 3 tablespoons of white vinegar
- 12 cardamom pods, bashed

Cooking Instructions:

1. Add all of the marinade ingredients into your blender except for the cardamom pods and blitz to a paste.
2. Add the paste with the cardamom pods to the chopped beef and set aside to marinade for at least 12 hours. Once the marinade is finished, add the ghee in your Instant Pot.
3. Press the Sauté function on your Instant Pot and heat the ghee. Add the onions for about 10 minutes until golden.
4. Add the beef with the marinade and brown for about 5 minutes. Add the rest of the ingredients into your Instant Pot.
5. Close and lock the lid in place. Select Manual, High Pressure for 35 minutes. When the timer beeps, do a natural pressure release for about 10 minutes.
6. Carefully remove the lid and remove the solids from the sauce with a slotted spoon. Press the Sauté function.
7. Cook, stirring occasionally until the sauce has thickened for a couple of minutes. Add the beef back into the sauce and stir to coat.
8. Serve immediately and enjoy!

Braised Korean Beef Ragu

Preparation time: 20 minutes

Cook time: 35 minutes

Total time: 55 minutes

Servings: 2

Calories: 373 kcal

Ingredients:

- 1 lb. of chuck roast, cubed

For the Sauce:

- 0.38 cup of low sodium soy sauce
- 0.13 cup of water
- 1.5 tbsp. of honey
- 0.5 tsp. of sesame oil
- 1 cloves garlic, minced
- 0.75 tbsp. of gochujang sauce

For the rest of the dish:

- Rotini pasta
- 1 tbsp. of arrowroot powder
- 1 tsp. of water
- Chopped scallions, for topping

Cooking Instructions:

1. Add the cubed chuck roast into the bottom of your Instant Pot. In a medium bowl, whisk together the sauce ingredients and pour over the beef.

2. Close and lock the lid in place. Select Manual, High Pressure for 35 minutes. Meanwhile, cook your pasta.
3. When the timer beeps, do a quick pressure release. Carefully open the lid and transfer the beef to a cutting board.
4. Shred the beef with two forks and set aside. Select the Sauté function and bring the pot to a boil.
5. Whisk together the arrowroot powder and water in a bowl. Pour the mixture into the Instant Pot and cook to thicken.
6. Return the beef back into the pot and stir to coat. Add the pasta or spoon the ragu over top of the pasta.
7. Sprinkle chopped scallions on top and serve!

Beef Curry

Preparation time: 10 minutes

Cook time: 39 minutes

Total time: 49 minutes

Servings: 2

Ingredients:

- 1 lb. of chuck roast or stew meat, cut into large chunks
- 0.5 large yellow onion, chopped
- 1 tbsp. of extra virgin olive oil
- 2 cloves fresh garlic, minced
- 1.5 cups of fresh water
- 0.5 tbsp. of Worcestershire sauce
- 0.25 large apple, grated or ¼ cup of apple sauce
- 1 tbsp. of clover honey, optional
- 1 tsp. of sea salt
- 0.5 cup of cremini mushrooms assorted
- 1 large potato, cut in quarters
- 2.5 large carrots, cut into 2 inch pieces
- 0.25 box of curry blocks, mix them up

Cooking Instructions:

1. Press the Sauté function on your Instant Pot and add the oil. Add the onions beef chunks and stir to coat.
2. Add the water, Worcestershire Sauce, garlic, salt, apple and honey. Close and lock the lid in place. Select Manual, High Pressure for 25 minutes.

3. When the timer beeps, do a natural pressure release for about 10 minutes. Carefully open the lid and drop in the curry blocks. Mix until melted.
4. Add the potatoes, carrots, mushrooms and give everything a good mix. Place the trivet and pour water inside the trivet and add the rice.
5. Close and lock the lid in place. Select Manual, High Pressure for 4 minutes. When the timer beeps, do a natural pressure release for about 10 minutes.
6. Carefully remove the lid. Serve over white rice and enjoy!

Braised Brisket

Preparation time: 5 minutes

Cook time: 55 minutes

Total time: 1 hour

Servings: 2

Ingredients:

- 1.50 pound of beef brisket, flat cut
- 2 tbsp. of canola oil
- 0.50 large onion, sliced
- 0.50 stalk celery, diced
- 0.50 carrot, chopped
- 0.50 tbsp. of tomato paste
- 1 cloves garlic, sliced
- 0.50 cup of red wine
- 0.50 cup of beef broth
- 0.50 bay leaf
- 1 sprigs fresh thyme

Cooking Instructions:

1. Take out the beef brisket fridge 30 minutes before cooking to bring meat to room temperature. Pat the meat dry with paper towel.
2. Generously season the meat with salt and pepper. Press the Sauté function on your Instant Pot and add t tbsp. of canola oil.
3. Add the brisket and cook, until browned on both side for about 4 minutes each. Remove and set aside. Add 2 tbsp. of canola oil, when oil begins to shimmer.
4. Add the onion, celery carrot and tomato paste. Cook for about 4 minutes, add the garlic and cook for additional 30 seconds.

5. Pour the red wine and remove any browned bits stuck to the bottom of the pot. Add the brisket on top of vegetables and add bay leaf and thyme.
6. Close and lock the lid in place. Select Manual, High Pressure for 55 minutes. When the timer beeps, do a natural pressure release for about 15 minutes.
7. Carefully open the lid and shred the meat. Press the Sauté function and cook, until the liquid is reduced by half. Ladle the sauce over brisket to serve.

Spicy Orange Beef

Preparation time: 10 minutes

Cook time: 12 minutes

Total time: 22 minutes

Serves: 2

Ingredients:

- 3 cloves garlic, minced
- 1 bell pepper, any color you desired, stem and seed removed and cut into strips
- 1 pound of flank steak, cut into ¼ strips
- ½ tablespoon of avocado oil
- ¾ cups of orange juice, fresh
- ¼ cup of coconut Amino or organic tamari
- 1 teaspoon of sesame oil
- ½ teaspoon of crushed red pepper flakes
- ½ teaspoon of orange zest
- 1 tablespoon of arrowroot powder
- 1.5 tablespoon of water, cold
- ½ bunch of green onions, chopped

Cooking Instructions:

1. Season the flank steak with salt and pepper. Press the Sauté function into the bottom of your Instant Pot and add the oil.
2. Sauté the meat in batches until browned and set aside. Add the garlic to the pot and sauté for about 1 minute.
3. Add the orange juice, soy sauce, sesame oil, red pepper flakes, and orange zest to the pot. Add the browned beef along with the juices.

4. Close and lock the lid in place. Select Manual, High Pressure for 12 minutes. When the timer beeps, do a quick pressure release.
5. Carefully open the lid and add the sliced bell peppers. In a medium bowl, combine together the arrowroot, or cornstarch and water and whisk until smooth.
6. Pour the mixture to the sauce, stirring constantly. Press the Sauté function and bring the pot to a boil. Stir in green onions.
7. Ladle into serving bowl and garnish with additional orange zest, green onion and red pepper flakes if desired.
8. Serve over rice and enjoy!

Ethiopian Beef Stew

Preparation time: 5 minutes

Cook time: 30 minutes

Total time: 35 minutes

Servings: 2

Calories: 461kcal

Ingredients:

- 0.75 pound of beef stew meat

- 1.5 tbsp. of ghee or butter

- 0.5 medium onion, chopped

- 0.5 tbsp. of ginger-garlic crushed, ½ inch ginger + 2 cloves garlic OR ½ tsp. of ginger powder + ½ tsp. of garlic powder

- 0.5 tbsp. of fried onions, optional

- 1.5 tbsp. of tomato paste

- 0.25 tsp. of sugar

- 0.5 tsp. of salt

- 0.75 tbsp. of Berbere seasoning

- 1 tsp. of coriander powder, substitute for Berbere seasoning (skip coriander above too)

- 0.13 tsp. of turmeric powder

- 0.5 tbsp. of garam masala

- 0.5 tbsp. of coriander powder

- 0.5 tsp. of ground cumin

- 0.13 tsp. of ground nutmeg

- 1 tsp. of smoked paprika

- 0.13 tsp. of cayenne pepper

- 0.13 tsp. of black pepper

- 0.5 cup of water

Cooking Instructions:

1. Pulse the onion chunks and ginger-garlic for about 8 to 10 times with a mini food processor. Select the Sauté function on your Instant Pot and add the ghee or butter.
2. Add the chopped onion, ginger-garlic, turmeric and salt and cook for about 4 minutes to caramelize. Add all dry spices, tomato paste and ¼ cup water.
3. Give everything a good stir and cook for about 1 minute. Add the rest of the water and beef cubes into the pot. Press the Cancel function.
4. Close and lock the lid in place. Select the Meat/Stew function for about 30 minutes. When the timer beeps, do a natural pressure release for about 10 minutes.
5. Carefully remove the lid and adjust the seasoning to your desired taste. Add sugar if desired.
6. Serve with a garden salad dressed with fresh lemon vinaigrette and enjoy!

STEW MEALS

Brunswick Stew

Preparation time: 10 minutes

Cook time: 25 minutes

Total time: 35 minutes

Serves: 2

Ingredients:

- ½ (7.5 oz.) pkg. chopped tomatoes (such as Pomì)
- ¼ lb. of Yukon Gold potatoes (about 1 large potatoes), cut into 1-inch cubes
- 1 cup of chopped Vidalia onion
- ½ cup of packed light brown sugar
- 6 tbsp. of Worcestershire sauce
- ¾ cup of apple cider vinegar
- ¾ cup of Dijon mustard
- 2 tbsp. of chopped fresh thyme
- ¾ tbsp. of kosher salt
- ¾ tbsp. of tomato paste
- ½ tsp. of unsweetened cocoa
- ¾ tsp. of crushed red pepper
- ½ (2 lb.) whole chicken
- 1 cup of frozen lima beans
- 1 cup of fresh or frozen corn kernels (about 2 ears)

- ¾ tsp. of black pepper

- 1/8 cup of thinly sliced scallions (about 1 scallions)

Cooking Instructions:

1. Add the tomatoes, potatoes, onion, Worcestershire sauce, vinegar, mustard, thyme, salt, tomato paste, cocoa, and red pepper into the Instant Pot.
2. Add the chicken on top of tomato mixture. Close and lock the lid in place. Select Manual, High Pressure for 25 minutes.
3. When the timer beeps, do a quick pressure release. Carefully open the lid and transfer chicken to a bowl.
4. Stir in tomato mixture into the pot and bring the pot to a boil. Stir in lima beans, corn, and black pepper; cook for about 2 minutes until the vegetables are cooked through.
5. Shred the chicken and discard the chicken skin. Pick the chicken meat from bones. Discard bones, and stir chicken meat and scallions into tomato mixture.
6. Serve and enjoy!

White Bean, Chickpea, and Tomato Stew

Preparation time: 10 minutes

Cook time: 15 minutes

Total time: 25 minutes

Servings: 2

Ingredients:

- 1/3 cup of dried chickpeas
- 1/3 cup of dried white beans, such as Great Northern or cannellini
- 2/3 tbsp. of olive oil
- 1/3 medium yellow onion, chopped
- 2/3 medium ribs celery, sliced
- ½ tsp. of dried dill
- ½ tsp. of ground cinnamon
- ½ tbsp. of mild paprika
- ½ tsp. of ground cumin
- 1/3 tsp. of salt
- 1/6 tsp. of ground black pepper
- Zero point three, 3 14 oz. can no-salt-added diced tomatoes, with their juices
- 1/12 cup of dried red lentils
- 1/12 cup of dried (medium-coarse) bulgur
- 2/3 tbsp. of tomato paste
- 11/12 cup of no-salt-added vegetable broth

Cooking Instructions:

1. Add the chickpeas in a bowl and the beans in a separate bowl. Cover each of the bowls with a few inches of water and soak for at least 8 hours.
2. Press the Sauté function and add the oil. Add the onion and celery; cook, stirring constantly for about 4 minutes, or until softened.
3. Stir in the dill, cinnamon, paprika, cumin, salt and pepper; and sauté for additional 20 seconds, or until fragrant. Drain the chickpeas and beans and add them into the bottom of your Instant Pot.
4. Add the canned tomatoes along with their juices, the lentils, and bulgur and tomato paste, and give everything a good stir until the paste is dissolved. Stir in the broth.
5. Close and lock the lid in place. Select Manual, High Pressure for 25 minutes. When the timer beeps, do a natural pressure release for about 15 minutes.
6. Carefully remove the lid and give everything a good stir. Ladle into individual bowls and serve immediately.
7. Serve and enjoy!

Tortilla Chicken Verde Chili

Preparation time: 5 minutes

Cook time: 20 minutes

Total time: 35 minutes

Serves: 2

Ingredients:

- ½ pound of chicken (boneless, skinless) thighs or rotisserie chicken meat (skinless)
- 1 tablespoon of olive oil or avocado oil
- ¾ - ½ teaspoon of ground cumin, divided
- ½ teaspoon of minced garlic
- ½ cup of chopped onion
- ½ cup of chopped bell pepper
- ½ cup of salsa verde
- Sea salt and black pepper to taste
- Optional garlic powder
- 2 oz. of green chiles
- ½ cups of chicken broth
- 1 ½ chopped medium gluten free tortillas (or corn tortillas) chopped
- Optional Extra Veggie mix-ins – ¾ cups of chopped cauliflower (or riced) or corn.
- Organic gluten free corn chips, optional for topping

Cooking Instructions:

1. Press the Sauté function on your Instant Pot and add the olive oil. Add the chicken, cumin, minced garlic, and chopped onion.

2. Cook the chicken for about 6 minutes or until no longer pink. Press the Cancel function and shred the chicken with two forks.
3. Add in the chopped bell pepper, optional chopped cauliflower or corn and the rest of the ingredients. Give everything a good mix.
4. Close and lock the lid in place. Select Manual, High Pressure for 10 minutes. When the timer beeps, do a natural pressure release for about 10 minutes.
5. Carefully remove the lid and mix again. Serve with slices jalapeno, crumbled Mexican cheese, splash of lime, lime slices and organic yellow corn chips to top.

Italian Sausage Stew

Preparation time: 15 minutes

Cook time: 15 minutes

Total time: 30 minutes

Servings: 2

Ingredients:

- 0.5 tablespoon of butter
- 0.13 pound of pastured ground pork, grass fed ground beef is great too
- 0.13 teaspoon of onion powder
- 0.13 teaspoon of garlic powder
- 0.38 teaspoon of basil
- 0.13 teaspoon of thyme
- 0.06 teaspoon of cumin
- 0.13 teaspoon of marjoram
- 0.06 teaspoon of cayenne
- 0.25 teaspoon of sea salt
- 0.06 teaspoon of black pepper
- 0.25 medium onion, diced
- 0.5 carrots, diced
- 0.5 stalks of celery, diced
- 1 cloves of garlic, minced
- 0.13 cup of white wine
- 0.25 - 3.75 ounces can organic diced tomatoes

- 0.5 quarts of bone broth

- 0.5-0.75 large handfuls kale, chopped

- 2 ounces of gluten free noodles, We like Tinkyada brand

- Sea salt and pepper to taste

- Freshly grated parm or other raw cheese to garnish

Cooking Instructions:

1. Press the Sauté function on your Instant Pot and add the butter to melt. Add the pork and all of the seasonings.
2. Give everything a good stir to combine and coat the meat. Add the onion, carrot, celery, and garlic, combine and sauté for about 5 minutes or until the veggies are soft.
3. Add the white wine and remove any browned bits stuck to the bottom of the pot. Add the diced tomatoes, broth, kale and noodles and stir to combine.
4. Close and lock the lid in place. Select Manual, High Pressure for 3 minutes. When the timer beeps, do a quick pressure release.
5. Carefully remove the lid and season with salt and pepper. Serve with freshly grated parmesan and enjoy!

Chicken & Smoked Sausage Stew

Serves: 2

Ingredients:

- ½ lb. of boneless, skinless chicken thighs
- ½ lb. of andouille pork sausage
- ½ tbsp. of coconut oil
- 3 cups of chopped tomatoes
- ½ medium white onion, diced
- 1 stalks celery, chopped
- 1 bell peppers, diced
- 1 large carrots, chopped
- 1 cup of bone broth or water
- 1/8 cup of parsley, minced
- 2 cloves garlic, minced
- ½ tsp. of salt
- ½ tsp. of thyme
- ¼ tsp. of smoked paprika
- ¼ tsp. of crushed red chili flakes
- 1/8 tsp. of black pepper
- 1/8 tsp. of cayenne
- ½ bay leaf
- Hot sauce to taste, optional

Cooking Instructions:

1. Press the Sauté function on your Instant Pot and add the coconut oil. Add the chicken and sausage and sauté for about 4 minutes per side.
2. Remove the meat from the pot, and set aside. Add the vegetables to the pot and cook, stirring occasionally. Add the minced garlic, broth and chopped tomatoes.
3. Bring the mixture to a simmer. Slice the chicken and sausage into bite-sized pieces. Add them back into the pot along with their spices.
4. Add the minced parsley and give everything a good stir. Close and lock the lid in place. Select the Soup function to cook for about 5-10 minutes.
5. When the timer beeps, do a quick pressure release. Carefully remove the lid and stir. Serve warm with hot sauce and enjoy!

Chocolatey Beef Stew

Preparation time: 10 minutes

Cook time: 25 minutes

Total time: 35 minutes

Ingredients:

- ½ onion, chopped
- 1 clove of garlic, chopped
- ½ stalk of celery, chopped
- Extra virgin olive oil
- ½ tin of plum tomatoes
- 75 ml of vegetable stock
- 50 ml of red wine
- 300 g of beef, diced
- 3.5 g porcini
- 140 g of mushrooms, quartered
- 110 g of carrots, sliced in half cm coins
- 20 g Lindt 85% chocolate (2 squares)

Cooking Instructions:

1. Select the Sauté function on your Instant Pot and a little drop of olive oil. Add the onion, garlic and celery. Add the beef and cook until browned.
2. Add red wine and remove any browned bits stuck to the bottom of the pot. Add the remaining ingredients. Close and lock the lid in place.
3. Select Manual, High Pressure for 25 minutes. When the timer beeps, do a natural pressure release for about 15 minutes.
4. Carefully remove the lid and give everything a good stir. Press the Sauté function and cook until the liquid is reduced by half.
5. Serve with mashed potatoes and enjoy!

Butter Chicken Curry

Preparation time: 5 minutes

Cook time: 14 minutes

Total time: 19 minutes

Servings: 2

Ingredients:

- 0.5 lb. of boneless, skinless chicken thighs, cut into bite-size pieces
- 1 tbsp. of butter, or ghee
- 0.25 medium onion, chopped
- 2-2.5 cloves garlic, minced
- 0.5 tbsp. of fresh grated ginger
- 0.25 tbsp. of curry powder
- 0.5 tsp. of garam masala
- 0.25 tsp. of salt
- 0.19 tsp. of smoked paprika
- 3.75 oz. of tomato sauce
- 0.25 cup of heavy cream
- Chopped cilantro, for garnish

Cooking Instructions:

1. Press the Sauté function on your Instant Pot and add the butter to melt. Add the chopped onions, garlic, ginger, and all spices.
2. Sauté the ingredients for about 5 minutes, stirring constantly. Press the Cancel function once the onion have softened.
3. Add the chopped chicken thighs and canned tomato sauce. Close and lock the lid in place. Select Manual, High Pressure for 7 minutes.

4. When the timer beeps, do a quick pressure release. Carefully open the lid and stir in the heavy cream.
5. Select the Sauté again and simmer for 2 minutes to thicken the sauce. Sprinkle with chopped cilantro.
6. Serve with basmati rice and enjoy!

Beef Masala Curry

Preparation time: 10 minutes

Cook time: 30 minutes

Total time: 40 minutes

Serves: 2

Ingredients:

- 1 pound of stewing beef, cut in 2 inch cubes
- ½ medium onion, chopped
- 1 ½ garlic cloves, minced
- ¼ cup of crushed tomatoes
- 1/8 cup of fresh cilantro, chopped
- ½ teaspoon of salt
- ½ teaspoon of freshly ground black pepper
- ½ teaspoon of turmeric
- ½ tablespoon of garam masala
- ¼ teaspoon of cumin
- ¼ teaspoon of coriander
- ¼ teaspoon of cayenne pepper
- ¼ teaspoon of smoked paprika
- ¼ teaspoon of lemon zest
- ½ teaspoon of brown sugar
- ½ tablespoon of oil
- ½ cup of beef stock

Cooking Instructions:

1. Press the Sauté function on your Instant Pot and add the oil. Add the chopped onions, garlic, spices, salt and pepper.
2. Sauté, for about 3 minutes or until onions become softened. Stir in the crushed tomatoes, brown sugar and bring to a boil.
3. Pour the ingredients into your food processor and blend all into a paste. Cook the meat to brown on both sides, pour in the blended spice paste, stock and add lemon zest.
4. Close and lock the lid in place. Select Manual, High Pressure for 30 minutes. When the timer beeps, do a quick pressure release. Carefully remove the lid.
5. Serve with steamed rice and chopped cilantro.

Venison Stew

Serves: 2

Ingredients:

- ½ pound of venison or Elk, cubed
- ½ tbsp. of olive or canola oil
- 1 rib celery, sliced
- ½ medium onion, diced
- ½ cup of pearl onions
- 1 medium carrots, sliced
- ½ clove garlic, minced
- ½ tsp. of onion powder
- ½ tsp. of seasoned salt
- ½ cup of dry red wine (pinot noir or cabernet sauvignon)
- ½ cup of beef broth
- 2 large potatoes, diced into 1-inch
- ¼ teaspoon of fresh chopped rosemary or a dash crumbled dry
- 1 tbsp. of flour
- 1 tbsp. of butter

Cooking Instructions:

1. Trim stew beef and cut them into bite sized pieces. Press the Sauté function on your Instant Pot and add the oil. Sauté the meat until golden on both sides.
2. Remove the meat and set aside. Add the onions, carrots, celery, garlic, onion powder and seasoned salt and cook for about 3 minutes or until the onions start to soften.
3. Pour the red wine and remove any browned bits stuck to the bottom of the pot. Add the meat, and beef broth.

4. Give everything a good stir and place the potatoes on top and sprinkle with rosemary. Close and lock the lid in place.
5. Select Manual, High Pressure for about 15-20 minutes. When the timer beeps, do a natural pressure release for about 10 minutes.
6. Carefully remove the lid. Meanwhile, melt the butter in a small sauce pan and stir in the flour. Add the butter mixture and simmer for about 5 minutes.
7. Serve and enjoy!

Kimchi Stew

Preparation time: 10 minutes

Cook time: 3 minutes

Total time: 13 minutes

Serves: 4

Ingredients:

- 1.5 cups of chopped sour kimchi
- ½ pound of pork belly, cut into 1.5 inch sized pieces (or pork shoulder cut into small pieces)
- ½ medium onion, sliced
- Dash of cooking oil
- ¾ cup of kimchi juice
- 1 tbsp. of red pepper paste
- ½ tbsp. of red pepper flakes
- ½ tbsp. of sugar
- 2 cups of water
- ½ package of firm tofu, sliced
- 1 green onions, chopped (for garnish)
- ½ tsp. of sesame oil

Broth packet:

- 2 whole garlic cloves
- 2 small square (about 2 inches in length) sheets of dried kelp
- 2 dried anchovies

Cooking Instructions:

1. Prepare the broth packet by using a disposable tea packet. Add the garlic, dried kelp, and dried anchovies in the packet and set aside.
2. Select the Sauté function on your Instant Pot and add the cooking oil. Add the pork and cook for about 2 minutes to brown on both sides.
3. Add the kimchi and onions. Sauté for additional couple of minutes. Add 2 cups of water and ¾ cup of kimchi juice. Add the sugar, red pepper flakes, and red pepper paste.
4. Close and lock the lid in place. Select the Meat/Stew function to cook for about 20 minutes. When the timer beeps, do a quick pressure release.
5. Carefully remove the lid and add the broth packet, and tofu. Press everything down the pot with a spoon. Close and lock the lid in place.
6. Select the Meat/Stew function to cook for about 3 minutes. When the timer beeps, do a quick pressure release.
7. Carefully open the lid and discard the broth packet. Add the sesame oil. Ladle into individual bowls and add the green onions on top.
8. Serve with rice and enjoy!

PORK MEALS

Pork Poblano Skillet Enchiladas

Preparation time: 20 minutes

Cook time: 1 hour 30 minutes

Total time: 1 hour 50 minutes

Servings: 2

Calories: 722 kcal

Ingredients:

For the pork:

- 0.83 lb. of boneless pork shoulder
- 5 oz. roasted salsa verde (jarred)

For the rest of the dish:

- 1 roasted poblanos, seeds removed and diced
- 5.17 oz. can of black beans, drained and rinsed
- 0.33 cup of frozen corn, thawed
- Salt and pepper, to taste
- 2 flour tortillas, cut lengthwise into thick 2" strips then halved
- 0.25 cup of shredded Colby jack cheese

Cooking Instructions:

1. Add the whole pork shoulder into the bottom of your Instant Pot and pour the salsa verde on top. Close and lock the lid in place.
2. Select the Meat button to cook for 65 minutes. When the timer beeps, do a natural pressure release for about 10 minutes.
3. Carefully open the lid and transfer the pork on to a cutting board and shred it with two forks. Preheat oven to broil the pork.

4. In a large, oven-safe skillet over medium-high heat, add the diced poblanos, beans, corn, and shredded pork.
5. Season with salt and pepper and cook until the ingredients are cooked through. Add the flour tortillas and add about ½ cup - 2/3 cup of the salsa verde liquid.
6. Stir to soften the tortillas and coat the ingredients. Sprinkle cheese on top and broil in the oven until cheese is melted. Garnish with green onions, if desired and serve.
7. Serve immediately and enjoy!

Pork Chops with Gravy

Preparation time: 10 minutes

Cook time: 8 minutes

Total time: 38 minutes

Servings: 2

Calories: 374kcal

Ingredients:

- 2 thick cut pork chops
- 0.38 teaspoon of salt
- 0.25 teaspoon of black pepper
- 0.25 teaspoon of garlic powder
- 1 tablespoon of oil
- 1 tablespoon of unsalted butter
- 0.5 yellow onion, chopped
- 0.25 red bell pepper, chopped
- 0.25 green bell pepper, chopped
- 0.5 tablespoon of garlic, minced
- 0.5 tablespoon of Worcestershire Sauce
- 0.5 tablespoon of steak sauce
- 0.5 tablespoon of hot sauce
- 0.5 tablespoon of Ketchup
- 0.5 teaspoon of dried thyme
- 0.38 cup of chicken broth

- 1 tablespoon of cornstarch

- 1 tablespoon of water

Cooking Instructions:

1. Generously season the pork chops with salt, pepper, and garlic powder on both sides. Select the "Sauté" function on your Instant Pot and add the olive oil.
2. Add the seasoned pork chops and sauté for to brown on each side for about 3 minutes. Remove the pork from Instant Pot and set aside.
3. Add the butter to melt. Add the onion and bell peppers and give everything a good stir. Add the garlic and cook, stirring occasionally until onions have softened, for about 2 minutes.
4. Pour the chicken broth into the pot and remove any browned bits stuck to the bottom of the pot. Add the Worcestershire sauce, steak sauce, hot sauce, ketchup, and thyme and stir.
5. Return the pork chops back into the pot, and place them on top of the liquid. Close and lock the lid in place. Select Manual, High Pressure for 8 minutes.
6. When the timer beeps, do a natural pressure release for about 10 minutes, then quick release any remaining pressure. Carefully open the lid and remove the pork chops.
7. Select the "Sauté" function and bring the pot to a boil. In a medium bowl, whisk together about ½ tablespoon of cornstarch and ½ tablespoon of water.
8. Pour the mixture it into the pot, while stirring. Give everything a good stir until thickened, for about 1 minute. Pour the gravy over the pork chops.
9. Serve and enjoy!

Baby Back Pork Ribs

Preparation time: 10 minutes

Cook time: 35 minutes

Total time: 45 minutes

Serves: 2

Ingredients:

- 1 (1.5 – 2 pounds) rack of baby back pork ribs
- ¾ cup of brown sugar
- 1 tablespoon of chili powder
- 1 teaspoon of dried parsley
- ½ teaspoon of salt
- ½ teaspoon of pepper
- ½ teaspoon of cumin
- ½ teaspoon of garlic powder
- ½ teaspoon of onion powder
- ¾ teaspoon of cayenne pepper
- ½ cup of water
- ¾ cup of apple cider vinegar
- ¾ teaspoon of liquid smoke, optional
- ¾ cup of BBQ sauce

Cooking Instructions:

1. Use a butter knife to remove the lining from the bottom side of the ribs under the skin. Pat dry with a paper towel.

2. In a medium bowl, combine together the brown sugar, chili powder, parsley, salt, pepper, cumin, garlic powder, onion powder and cayenne pepper.
3. Rub the mixture all over the ribs. Place the steamer rack into the bottom of your Instant Pot and place the ribs on top of the rack, standing on their side.
4. Pour in the water, apple cider and liquid smoke, if desired. Close and lock the lid in place. Select the Meat function to cook for 25 minutes.
5. When the timer beeps, do a natural pressure release for about 10 minutes, then quick release any remaining pressure.
6. Carefully open the lid and transfer the ribs on a foil lined baking sheet. Brush down with your desired BBQ sauce. Broil the ribs for about 5 minutes.
7. Serve and enjoy!

Ginger Pork Shogayaki

Preparation time: 5 minutes

Cook time: 50 minutes

Total time: 55 minutes

Serving: 2

Ingredients:

- 1 lb. of pork shoulder
- 1 medium onion, chopped
- 1 tbsp. of peanut oil
- ½ - 1 head romaine lettuce
- Green onions, finely chopped, optional for garnish
- Kosher salt and ground black pepper to taste

Ginger Garlic Sauce:

- 1 - 2 tbsp. of ginger root, finely grated
- 1 clove garlic, finely grated
- 1 tbsp. of Japanese soy sauce
- ½ tbsp. of white miso paste (optional) or 1 additional tbsp. of soy sauce
- 2 tbsp. of Japanese cooking sake
- 2 tbsp. of mirin (Japanese sweet cooking rice wine)
- ¼ cup of water

Pot-in-Pot Rice:

- 1 cup of medium grain Calrose rice
- 1 cup of cold water

Cooking Instructions:

1. Select the Sauté function on your Instant Pot. In a glass measuring cup, mix together all the ginger garlic sauce ingredients.
2. Season the pork shoulder meat with kosher salt and ground black pepper. Add 1 tablespoon of peanut oil into the bottom of your Instant Pot.
3. Add in the seasoned pork shoulder meat, and sauté to brown on each side for about 5 minutes. Transfer the pork to cool on a chopping board.
4. Select the Sauté function and add the chopped onions. Season with a pinch of kosher salt and ground black pepper. Cook for about 2 minutes or until soften.
5. Cut the pork shoulder meat into 0.5" thick slices. Pour a dash of ginger garlic sauce and remove any browned bits stuck to the bottom of the pot. Pour in the rest of the ginger garlic sauce.
6. Add the sliced pork shoulder meat along with the juices into the Instant Pot. Place the steamer rack into the pot and add 1 cup (230g) Calrose rice and 1 cup of cold water.
7. Close and lock the lid in place. Select Manual, High Pressure for 6 minutes. When the timer beeps, do a natural pressure release for about 10 minutes.
8. Carefully remove the lid fluff the rice and set aside. Adjust the seasoning with more soy sauce if desired.
9. Serve over Calrose rice with the chopped romaine lettuce. Garnish with finely chopped green onions.
10. Serve immediately and enjoy!

Bacon Wrapped Pork

Preparation time: 10 minutes

Cook time: 15 minutes

Total time: 25 minutes

Servings: 2

Ingredients:

- ½ Smithfield All Natural Boneless Loin Filet
- 2.5 slices of thick cut bacon
- 2 sprigs thyme
- 2 sprigs rosemary
- ½ cup of balsamic vinegar
- ½ tablespoon of Worcestershire sauce
- ¼ tablespoon of soy sauce
- 1 tablespoon of brown sugar
- 1 cloves garlic, minced
- ½ teaspoon of salt
- ¼ teaspoon of garlic powder
- ¼ teaspoon of pepper
- ½ tablespoon of canola oil

Cooking Instructions:

1. Press the Sauté function on your Instant Pot and add the olive oil. Season the pork on both sides with salt, pepper, and garlic powder.
2. Lay fresh herbs on loin. Wrap the pieces of bacon around the pork. Add the pork into the pot and sauté for about 2-3 minutes or until browned.

3. Meanwhile, mix together the balsamic vinegar, brown sugar, Worcestershire sauce, soy sauce, and minced garlic.
4. Once pork is browned on one side, turn on the other side and sauté for about 2-3 minutes or until browned. Add balsamic mixture.
5. Close and lock the lid in place. Select Manual, High Pressure for 10 minutes. When the timer beeps, do a natural pressure release for about 10 minutes.
6. Carefully remove the lid and give everything a good stir. Serve immediately and enjoy!

Cafe Rio Pork

Preparation time: 10 minutes

Cook time: 30 minutes

Total time: 40 minutes

Servings: 2

Calories: 387 kcal

Ingredients:

- 0.5 pound of boneless pork carnitas, shoulder, picnic or butt roast etc.
- 0.13 cup of coke, not diet
- 0.13 cup of brown sugar
- 0.38 cup of red enchilada sauce
- 1 ounces of diced green chilies
- 0.25 cup of water

Seasoning Mixture:

- 0.25 tablespoon of chili powder
- 0.13 tablespoon of cumin
- 0.25 teaspoon of garlic powder
- 0.13 teaspoon of basil
- 0.13 teaspoon of oregano
- 0.25 teaspoon of onion powder
- 0.25 teaspoon of salt
- 0.13 teaspoon of pepper
- 0.25 tablespoon of cornstarch, optional

- 0.25 tablespoon of water, optional

Cooking Instructions:

1. In a medium bowl, mix together the seasoning mixture. Cut the pork into 1-inch pieces and add them into a zippered plastic bag.
2. Add seasoning to pork and shake them to coat. Add the meat into the bottom of your Instant Pot. Pour 1 cup of water. Close and lock the lid in place.
3. Select Manual, High Pressure for 30 minutes. When the timer beeps, do a natural pressure release for about 10 minutes.
4. Carefully remove the lid and drain any excess liquid. In a separate bowl, mix together the coke, brown sugar, enchilada sauce and green chilies.
5. Pour the mixture over meat. Press the Sauté function and cook, stirring occasionally until sauce thickens.
6. Serve with rice and black beans and enjoy!

Sausage Gravy

Preparation time: 5 minutes

Cook time: 2 minutes

Total time: 17 minutes

Servings: 2

Calories: 383kcal

Ingredients:

- 0.33 pound of pork sausage
- 1 tablespoon of butter, unsalted
- 0.08 cup of All-purpose flour
- 1 cup of milk
- 0.33 tablespoon of maple syrup
- 0.67 teaspoon of salt
- 0.33 teaspoon of black pepper

Cooking Instructions:

1. Press the Sauté function on your Instant Pot and add the sausage. Sauté, stirring for about 5 minutes or until the sausage is no longer pink.
2. Add the butter and stir to melt the butter. Sprinkle the meat with flour and stir. Sauté for about 1 minute while stirring.
3. Add the milk, maple syrup, salt and black pepper. Remove any browned bits stuck to the bottom of the pot. Close and lock the lid in place.
4. Press the "Pressure Cook" function and adjust to cook on Low Pressure for about 2 minutes. When the timer beeps, do a quick pressure release.
5. Carefully remove the lid and stir the gravy. The gravy will thicken upon stirring. Press the Sauté function and cook until your desired thickness is achieved.
6. Serve and enjoy!

Pulled Pork

Preparation time: 30 mins

Cook time: 1 hour

Total time: 1 hour 30 minutes

Servings: 2

Calories: 266 kcal

Ingredients:

- 1 cloves garlic, peeled
- ¼ medium onion, cut into quarters
- ¼ chili mild
- ¼ small dried hot chili
- ½ tbsp. of dried oregano
- ½ tbsp. of lime juice or orange juice
- ¼ tbsp. of salt
- ½ tsp. of black pepper
- 1 tbsp. of oil divided
- 1 lb. about of pork shoulder, trimmed of excess fat

Cooking Instructions:

1. In a food processor or blender, add together the garlic, onion, chilies, oregano, lime juice, salt, pepper, and ½ tbsp. of oil and processes until to form a thick paste.
2. Cut the pork into half or smaller pieces to fit into the Instant Pot. Rub the marinade all over the pork. Cover and allow to marinate in the refrigerator for at least 1 hour - 24 hours.
3. When ready to cook, add the remaining ½ tbsp. of oil into the pot and add the pork shoulder. Place it down with the skin up if there's still skin on the pork.
4. Close and lock the lid in place. Select Manual, High Pressure for 60 minutes. When the timer beeps, do a natural pressure release for about 10 minutes.

5. Carefully remove the lid and shred the pork with two forks. Adjust the seasoning with more salt and pepper. Squeeze a little extra lime juice over the top.
6. Serve immediately and enjoy!

Honey Soy Pork Tenderloin

Preparation time: 5 minutes

Cook time: 25 minutes

Total time: 30 minutes

Servings: 2

Ingredients:

- 0.5 pound of pork tenderloin
- 0.11 cup of soy sauce
- 0.11 cup of water
- 0.08 cup of honey
- 0.33 tablespoon of ginger, minced
- 0.67 cloves garlic, minced
- 0.33 tablespoon of sesame oil
- 0.67 teaspoon of cornstarch
- Green onions, optional
- Sesame seeds, optional

Cooking Instructions:

1. Add together the soy sauce, water, honey, ginger, garlic, and sesame oil into the bottom of your Instant Pot. Add in the pork tenderloin.
2. Close and lock the lid in place. Select Manual, High Pressure for about 7 minutes. When the timer beeps, do a natural pressure release for about 7 minutes.
3. Carefully open the lid and remove pork. Press the Sauté function. In a medium bowl, combine together the cornstarch ½ teaspoon of water and pour into the pot.
4. Sauté, stirring for about 2 minutes or until thickened. Ladle thickened sauce over pork loin and top with green onions and sesame seeds.
5. Serve over cooked rice or zoodles and enjoy!

Pork Chile Verde

Preparation time: 10 minutes

Cook time: 35 minutes

Total time: 45 minutes

Servings: 2

Calories: 170 kcal

Ingredients:

- 0.5 pounds pork butt roast, cut into large pieces

Sauce Vegetables:

- 0.75 tomatillos, husks removed
- 0.75 jalapeno peppers
- 0.5 poblano peppers
- 1.5 cloves garlic
- 0.25 tomato, chopped
- 0.5 tsp. of roasted cumin powder
- Salt, to taste

Finishing Ingredients:

- 0.06 cup of cilantro
- 0.25 tbsp. of fish sauce

Cooking Instructions:

1. In a small sauce pan, add the cumin seeds and roast until just toasty-looking, and place on a paper towel to cool.
2. Add the pork and all sauce ingredients into the bottom of your Instant Pot, starting with the vegetables at the bottom. Place the cumin in a mortar and grind.

3. Sprinkle the pork with the cumin and salt. Close and lock the lid in place. Select Manual, High Pressure for 30 minutes.
4. When the timer beeps, do a natural pressure release for about 10 minutes. Carefully open the lid and remove pork chunks with tongs.
5. Add in cilantro and fish sauce. Puree the vegetables with an immersion blender. Add the pork back into the pot and stir.
6. Serve and enjoy!

Kalua Pork

Preparation time: 10 minutes

Cook time: 1 hour 30 minutes

Total time: 1 hour 40 minutes

Servings: 2

Calories: 403kcal

Ingredients:

- 1.25 lb. of pork butt (bone removed and cut into large chunks)
- 0.25 tbsp. of Alaea Hawaiian Sea Salt
- 0.25 tsp. of smoked paprika or liquid smoke
- 0.25 cup of water
- 0.25 head green cabbage, sliced

Cooking Instructions:

1. Cut the pork into large chunks and discard the bones. In a medium bowl, mix together the Alaea sea salt and smoked paprika.
2. Sprinkle the pork with salt mixture and rub in to thoroughly coat. Add the pork into the bottom of your Instant Pot and pour the water.
3. Close and lock the lid in place. Select Manual, High Pressure for 90 minutes. When the timer beeps, do a natural pressure release for about 15 minutes.
4. Carefully remove the lid and transfer the pork to a bowl. Add the sliced cabbage to the juices in the Instant Pot and give everything a good stir to coat.
5. Close and lock the lid in place. Select Manual, High Pressure for 3 minutes. When the timer beeps, do a natural pressure release for about 10 minutes.
6. Carefully remove the lid and add the cabbage to the pork and give everything a good stir to combine.
7. Serve with rice, Hawaiian potato salad, or on hamburger buns.

Boneless Pork Chops

Preparation time: 10 mins

Cook time: 7 mins

Total time: 17 mins

Serves: 2

Ingredients:

- 2 pork chops, boneless 1″ thick
- 2 tbsp. of brown sugar
- 1 tsp. of salt
- 1 tsp. of black pepper
- 1 tsp. of paprika
- ½ tsp. of onion powder
- 1 tablespoon of butter
- 1 cup of chicken broth
- ½ tbsp. of Worcestershire sauce
- 1 tsp. of Liquid Smoke

Cooking Instructions:

1. In a medium bowl, mix together the spices and brown sugar. Rub the mixture on both sides of pork chops.
2. Press the Sauté function on your Instant Pot and add the 1 tbsp. of butter. Once hot, add the pork chops and brown on all sides for about 2 minutes each.
3. Remove the pork chops and keep aside. Press the Cancel function. Pour 1 cup of chicken broth and remove any browned bits stuck to the bottom of the pot.
4. Add the Worcestershire sauce and liquid smoke. Add the pork chops on top of the liquid in the pot. Close and lock the lid in place.
5. Select Manual, High Pressure for 7 minutes. When the timer beeps, do a natural pressure release for about 15 minutes, then quick release any remaining pressure.

6. Carefully open the lid and remove the pork chops. Allow the pork chops to cool for a couple of minutes before serving.
7. Serve immediately and enjoy!

VEGETARIAN MEALS

Thai Butternut Squash Curry

Preparation time: 10 minutes

Cook time: 8 minutes

Total time: 18 minutes

Serves: 2

Ingredients:

- 0.11 cup of Thai Red curry paste
- 1 can (7 oz.) coconut milk
- 1 cup of low sodium veggie broth
- ¼ tsp. of fish sauce
- ¼ tbsp. of creamy peanut butter
- 1 cup of cubed butternut squash
- ¼ stick of cinnamon
- ½ inch fresh ginger, grated
- Juice from half lime
- ½ cup of shredded kale
- ½ lb. of wide egg noodles, such as tagliatelle
- ¾ cup of fresh cilantro, or basil, chopped
- ¼ pomegranate, arils for serving

Cooking Instructions:

1. Combine together the curry paste, coconut milk, 1 cup broth, fish sauce, and peanut butter into the bottom of your Instant Pot.

2. Add the butternut squash, cinnamon, ginger, and lime juice. Season with salt and pepper. Close and lock the lid in place.
3. Select Manual, High Pressure for about 8 minutes. When the timer beeps, do a quick pressure release. Press the Sauté function on your Instant Pot.
4. Carefully remove the lid and stir in the kale. Sauté for about 5 minutes or until wilted. Stir in the cilantro or basil, if desired. Add broth if the curry seems too thick.
5. Bring a large pot of salted water to a boil and add the noodles. Cook the noodles according to package directions.
6. Divide the noodles among bowls and spoon the curry on top. Top with pomegranate arils and cilantro.
7. Serve and enjoy!

Vegetable Soup

Serves: 2

Preparation time: 10 minutes

Cook time: 12 minutes

Total time: 45 minutes

Ingredients:

- ¼ tablespoon of extra-virgin olive oil
- ¼ medium onion, chopped
- 1 garlic cloves, minced
- Kosher salt
- Freshly ground black pepper
- ¼ tablespoon of tomato paste
- ½ cup of chopped cabbage
- ½ small cauliflower florets
- ½ carrots, sliced
- ½ celery stalks, sliced
- ¼ red bell pepper, chopped
- ¼ medium zucchini, chopped
- ½ (7 ounces) can kidney beans, rinsed and drained
- ½ (7 ounces) can diced tomatoes
- 1 cup of low-sodium vegetable broth
- ½ teaspoon of Italian seasoning
- ¼ teaspoon of paprika

- Freshly chopped parsley, for serving

Cook Instructions:

1. Press the Sauté function on your Instant Pot and add the extra virgin oil. Add the onion, and garlic. Season with salt and pepper.
2. Sauté, stirring occasionally for about 5 minutes or until onion softens. Add the tomato paste and cook, stirring for additional 1 minute.
3. Add the rest of the ingredients and give everything a good stir to combine. Close and lock the lid in place. Select Manual, High Pressure for about 12 minutes.
4. When the timer beeps, do a quick pressure release. Carefully open the lid and stir. Season with salt and pepper.
5. Garnish with parsley and a drizzle of olive oil before serving. Serve and enjoy!

Mashed Sweet Potatoes with Garlic and Rosemary

Preparation time: 10 minutes

Cook time: 15 minutes

Total time: 25 minutes

Servings: 2

Calories: 204 kcal

Ingredients:

- 0.25 cup of water
- A pinch of salt
- 0.75 lb. of sweet potatoes peeled and cut into 2" x 2" pieces
- 1.5 medium cloves garlic, peeled
- 0.25 tsp. of kosher salt
- 3.75 - 5 turns of freshly ground black pepper
- 0.75 tablespoon of vegan butter
- A pinch ground cinnamon
- 0.06 cup of coconut milk (canned)
- 0.13 tsp. of fresh rosemary leaves, chopped

Cooking Instructions:

1. Add the sweet potato pieces into the steamer basket. Place the steamer basket into the bottom of your Instant Pot along with water.
2. Add a pinch of salt and whole garlic cloves. Close and lock the lid in place. Select Manual, High Pressure for 15 minutes.
3. When the timer beeps, do a quick pressure release. Carefully open the lid and transfer the steamed sweet potatoes to a large mixing bowl.
4. Mash the cooked potatoes with a large fork or a potato masher.
5. Add the salt, freshly ground black pepper, vegan butter, pinch of cinnamon, coconut milk and finely chopped rosemary leaves.

6. Continue mashing the sweet potatoes until your desired texture is achieved. Serve warm and enjoy!

Creamy Broccoli Mac and Cheese

Serves: 2

Preparation time: 15 minutes

Cook time: 20 minutes

Total time: 35 minutes

Ingredients:

- ½ lb. of fusilli pasta
- 1 tbsp. of unsalted butter
- A pinch of kosher salt
- Freshly ground black pepper, to taste
- 1 cup of broccoli florets
- ½ tsp. of Dijon mustard
- ¾ tsp. of garlic powder
- ½ (2.5 oz.) can evaporated milk
- ½ cup of half and half
- 4 oz. of extra sharp cheddar cheese, grated

Cooking Instructions:

1. Add the pasta, butter and salt into the bottom of your Instant Pot along with 1 ½ cups of water. Close and lock the lid in place.
2. Select Manual, High Pressure for 5 minutes. When the timer beeps, do a quick pressure release. Carefully open the lid and stir in broccoli.
3. Press the Sauté function. Cook stirring occasionally, for about 3 minutes or until the liquid has reduced by half. Stir in Dijon and garlic powder.
4. Press the Keep Warm function. Stir in milk and half and half until warmed for about 2 minutes. Whisk in the cheese and stir until melted. Season with salt and pepper.
5. Serve immediately and enjoy!

Steamed Artichokes

Preparation time: 5 minutes

Cook time: 20 minutes

Total time: 25 minutes

Serves: 2

Ingredients:

- 1 cup of water
- 3 cloves garlic
- 1 bay leaf
- 2-4 fresh large artichokes, trimmed
- 1 fresh lemon wedge

Cooking Instructions:

1. Pour the water, garlic cloves and bay leaf into the bottom of your Instant Pot, and place the steamer basket.
2. Rub the lemon wedge all over the outside of the trimmed artichokes. Add the artichokes in a single layer on top of the steamer basket.
3. Add the lemon wedge in the water. Close and lock the lid in place. Select Manual, High Pressure for 10 minutes. When the timer beeps, do a quick pressure release.
4. Carefully open the lid and transfer the artichokes to serving bowl with a pair of tongs.
5. Serve with your favorite dipping sauce and enjoy!

Cheesy Garlic Spaghetti Squash

Preparation time: 10 minutes

Cook time: 20 minutes

Total time: 1 hour

Servings: 2

Ingredients:

- 1 pound of spaghetti squash
- 2 tablespoons of butter
- 2 garlic cloves, minced
- ½ cup of broccoli florets cut into bite-sized pieces
- 1 tablespoon of chicken broth
- ¼ cup of grated Parmesan cheese, plus more for garnish
- ¼ cup of shredded mozzarella cheese
- Fresh ground black pepper

Cooking Instructions:

1. Pierce the squash all over with a sharp knife to make ½ inch cuts into the skin. Pour 1 cup of water into the bottom of your Instant Pot and place the trivet.
2. Place squash on trivet. Close and lock the lid in place. Select Manual, High Pressure for 15 minutes. When the timer beeps, do a quick pressure release.
3. Carefully open the lid and transfer the squash to a bowl to cool. Drain water from Instant Pot and press the Sauté button. Add in garlic and butter.
4. Sauté until butter is melted. Add in broccoli and broth and sauté until broccoli is tender. Press the Keep Warm button and slice squash in half.
5. Shred the squash with a fork. Add shredded squash into the bottom of your Instant Pot and add the cheese.
6. Toss squash in cheese until the cheese has coated and melted. Add more chicken broth if the mixture is too dry.
7. Garnish with fresh ground pepper and more Parmesan cheese if needed. Serve immediately and enjoy!

Spiced Quinoa and Cauliflower Rice Bowls

Preparation time: 10 minutes

Cook time: 1 minute

Total time: 11 minutes

Servings: 2

Ingredients:

- ½ tablespoon of olive oil
- ½ medium onion, chopped
- ¼ cup of uncooked quinoa, rinsed
- ½ garlic cloves, minced
- ¼ inch fresh ginger, grated
- ¼ teaspoon of ground turmeric
- ¼ teaspoon of ground cumin
- ¼ teaspoon of ground coriander
- ½ cups of vegetable broth, divided
- 4 ounces of firm tofu, cut into ½ inch cubes
- ½ bell peppers, chopped
- ½ pound (1 cup) cauliflower rice
- ¼ cup of fresh cilantro leaves
- ¼ cup of toasted sliced almonds
- 2 tablespoons of lemon juice
- Salt and pepper, to taste

Cooking Instructions:

1. Press the Sauté function on your Instant Pot and add the olive oil. Cook the onions until soft for about 2-3 minutes.
2. Add in quinoa, garlic, ginger and stir for additional 2 minutes. Stir in the spices along with salt and pepper, until fragrant, for about 30 seconds.
3. Pour the broth and remove any browned bits stuck to the bottom of the pot. Add in the tofu, bell pepper, and rest of the broth into the pot.
4. Give everything a good stir. Pres the Cancel function. Close and lock the lid in place. Select Manual, High Pressure for 1 minute.
5. When the timer beeps, do a natural pressure release for about 5 minutes, then quick release any remaining pressure.
6. Carefully remove the lid and stir in the cauliflower rice along with the remaining ingredients. Cover the lid and don't lock.
7. Allow it to rest for about 5 minutes to soften the cauliflower rice. Add in the sliced almond, fresh cilantro, lemon juice.
8. Give everything a good stir. Adjust the seasoning with more salt and pepper. Ladle into bowls and serve warm.
9. Serve immediately and enjoy!

Portobello Pot Roast

Preparation time: 10 minutes

Cook time: 20 minutes

Total time: 30 minutes

Servings: 2

Ingredients:

- 0.5 lb. of Yukon gold potatoes, cut into bite-sized pieces
- 0.75 lb. of baby Bella mushrooms (cut them in half)
- 2 large carrots, peeled and cut into bite-sized pieces
- 1 cup of frozen pearl onions
- 1 cloves of garlic, minced
- 1 sprigs fresh thyme
- 1 cup of vegetable stock, divided
- ¼ cup of dry red or white wine
- 1 tbsp. of tomato paste
- 1 tbsp. of (vegetarian) worcestershire
- ½ tbsp. of cornstarch
- Kosher salt and freshly-cracked black pepper
- Finely chopped fresh parsley, optional for garnish

Cooking Instructions:

1. Add together the potatoes, mushrooms, carrots, onions, garlic, thyme, vegetable stock, wine and worcestershire into the bottom of your Instant Pot.
2. Toss everything to combine. Close and lock the lid in place. Select Manual, High Pressure for 20 minutes.

3. When the timer beeps, do a natural pressure release for about 15 minutes. Carefully open the lid. Press the Sauté function on your Instant Pot.
4. In a medium bowl, whisk together the remaining vegetable stock and cornstarch until combined. Pour the roast mixture into the pot and gently toss to combine.
5. Sauté for about 2-3 minutes, until the sauce thickens to your desired texture. Serve immediately, garnished with fresh parsley if desired.

Vegetarian Chili

Preparation time: 5 minutes

Cook time: 30 minutes

Total time: 35 minutes

Serves: 2

Ingredients:

- ½ teaspoon of olive oil
- ¼ yellow onion, chopped
- 1 garlic cloves, minced
- ¾ cup of chili powder
- ½ teaspoon of dried oregano
- ½ teaspoon of ground cumin
- ¼ tablespoon of tomato paste
- ¼ cup of low sodium vegetable broth
- ¼ (7 ounces) can crushed tomatoes
- ¼ chipotle pepper, seeded & minced
- ¼ teaspoon of adobo sauce (from chipotle pepper can)
- ½ (4 ounces) cans black beans (reduced sodium), drained & rinsed
- ½ (4 ounces) cans red kidney beans (reduced sodium), drained & rinsed
- ½ (4 ounces) can cannellini or great northern beans (reduced sodium), drained & rinsed
- ¼ teaspoon of salt
- Chopped cilantro or flat-leaf parsley, if desired

Cooking Instructions:

1. Press the Sauté function on your Instant Pot and add the olive oil.
2. Add the onions and sauté, stirring occasionally for about 5 minutes or until softened.
3. Stir in the garlic, chili powder, oregano and cumin, and sauté for 1 minute. Add the tomato paste and sauté, stirring frequently for additional 1 minute.
4. Add the vegetable broth, crushed tomatoes, chipotle pepper, adobo sauce, black beans, red kidney beans, cannellini beans and salt, and give everything a good stir to combine.
5. Close and lock the lid in place. Select Manual, High Pressure for 10 minutes. When the time beeps, do a natural pressure release for about 5 minutes, then quick release any remaining pressure.
6. Carefully remove the lid and stir in the cilantro or parsley. Serve immediately and enjoy!

VEGAN MEALS

Mushroom Risotto

Preparation time: 15 minutes

Cook time: 15 minutes

Total time: 30 minutes

Servings: 2

Calories: 379kcal

Ingredients:

- 0.4 tbsp. of olive oil
- 0.8 tbsp. of vegan butter, divided
- 0.4 medium onion, diced
- 1.2 cloves garlic, minced
- 3.2 ounces of cremini mushrooms dry brushed & diced
- 0.3 tsp. of dried thyme
- 0.6 cups of Arborio rice
- 0.2 cup of dry white wine
- 1.6 cups of vegetable broth, low sodium
- 0.5 tsp. of sea salt, more to taste
- Fresh ground pepper to taste
- 0.4 cup of frozen peas, thawed
- 1.2-1.6 tbsp. of Vegan Parmesan Cheese, optional

Cooking Instructions:

1. Press the Sauté function on your Instant Pot and add the olive oil and 0.8 tbsp. of butter. Once hot, add the onions and cook for about 2 minutes or until soften.
2. Add the garlic and thyme and cook for 1 minute. Add the mushrooms and cook for about 3-4 minutes or until tender.
3. Add the rice and give everything a good stir to coat. Pour in the wine and sauté for about 2 minutes. Stir in the broth, salt, and pepper.
4. Close and lock the lid in place. Select Manual, High Pressure for 6 minutes. When the timer beeps, do a quick pressure release. Carefully remove the lid and stir.
5. Stir in the peas, remaining butter, and vegan parmesan. Adjust the seasoning with salt and pepper.
6. Serve with fresh-cut parsley, crushed red pepper flakes, and fresh cracked pepper. Serve and enjoy!

Lentil Coconut Curry

Serves: 2

Preparation time: 10 minutes

Cook time: 15 minutes

Total time: 45 minutes

Ingredients:

- ½ cup of lentils, green or brown
- ¼ tbsp. of coconut oil
- ½ medium shallot, finely chopped
- 1.5 tbsp. of minced fresh ginger
- 1 tbsp. of minced garlic, about 3 cloves
- ½ tbsp. of curry powder, plus more ½ tsp.
- ¼ tbsp. of coconut sugar or brown sugar
- ½ tsp. of kosher salt
- 1/8 tsp. of ground turmeric
- 1/8 tsp. of cayenne pepper
- ½ can light coconut milk, about 7 ounces
- 1 tbsp. of freshly squeezed lemon juice, about ¼ large lemon
- Cooked brown rice, for serving
- Chopped fresh cilantro, for serving

Cooking Instructions:

1. Rinse and drain the lentils in a bowl and set aside. Press the Sauté function on your Instant Pot and add the coconut oil.

2. Once hot, add ½ tbsp. of water, the shallot, ginger, and garlic into the bottom of your Instant Pot. Sauté, stirring occasionally for about 2 minutes or until very fragrant and the shallot is soft.
3. Add the curry powder, coconut sugar, salt, turmeric, and cayenne and give everything a good stir. Add the lentils, coconut milk, and ½ cup of water.
4. Give everything a good stir to coat the lentils with the liquid. Press the Cancel function. Close and lock the lid in place.
5. Select Manual, High Pressure for 15 minutes. When the timer beeps, do a natural pressure release for about 10 minutes, then quick release any remaining pressure.
6. Carefully remove the lid and stir in the lemon juice. Adjust the seasoning to suit your desired taste. Add small water if the curry is too thick.
7. Serve warm with rice, sprinkled with cilantro.

Quinoa Burrito Bowls

Preparation time: 5 minutes

Cook time: 20 minutes

Total time: 25 minutes

Servings: 2

Calories: 163 kcal

Ingredients:

- 0.5 tsp. of extra-virgin olive oil
- 0.25 red onion, diced
- 0.5 bell pepper, diced
- 0.25 tsp. of salt
- 0.5 tsp. of ground cumin
- 0.5 cup of quinoa, rinsed well
- 0.5 cup of prepared salsa
- 0.5 cup of water
- 0.75 cup of cooked black beans, or 1 (15 ounces) can, drained and rinsed
- Optional toppings: Avocado, guacamole, fresh cilantro, green onions, salsa, lime wedges, shredded lettuce

Cooking Instructions:

1. Press the Sauté function on your Instant Pot and add the oil. Add the onions and peppers. Cook the ingredients for about 5 minutes or until they begin to soften.
2. Add in cumin and salt and cook for additional 1 minute. Press the Cancel function. Add in the quinoa, salsa, water, and beans.
3. Close and lock the lid in place. Select the Rice function and adjust to cook on Low Pressure for about 12 minutes.
4. When the timer beeps, do a natural pressure release for about 15 minutes. Carefully remove the lid and fluff the quinoa with a fork.

5. Serve hot with your favorite toppings like: avocado, diced onions, salsa, and shredded lettuce.

Cauliflower Tikka Masala

Preparation time: 10 minutes

Cook time: 2 minutes

Total time: 12 minutes

Servings: 2

Ingredients:

- ½ tablespoon of vegan butter (or oil)
- ½ small onion, diced
- 1.5 cloves of garlic, minced
- ½ tablespoon of freshly grated ginger
- 1 teaspoon of dried fenugreek leaves
- 1 teaspoon of garam masala
- ½ teaspoon of turmeric
- ¼ teaspoon of ground chili
- 1/8 teaspoon of ground cumin
- ¼ teaspoon of salt
- ½ 14 oz. can diced tomatoes with their juice (about 1.5 cups)
- ½ tablespoon of maple syrup
- ½ small cauliflower head, cut into florets (about 2 cups florets)
- ¼ cup (59ml) non-dairy yogurt (or cashew cream)
- Optional toppings: fresh parsley, roasted cashews

Cooking Instructions:

1. Press the Sauté function on your Instant Pot and add the oil. Add the onion, garlic, and ginger and sauté for about 3-4 minutes, or until the onions becomes soft.
2. Add the dried fenugreek leaves, garam masala, turmeric, chili, cumin, and salt. Sauté for additional 2 minutes, stirring constantly.
3. Add few tablespoons of water and remove any browned bits stuck to the bottom of the pot. Add the crushed tomatoes, maple syrup, and cauliflower florets.
4. Close and lock the lid in place. Select Manual, High Pressure for 2 minutes. When the timer beeps, do a natural pressure release for about 10 minutes.
5. Carefully remove the lid and stir in the non-dairy yogurt. Give everything a good stir to combine.
6. Serve warm with rice, naan, or tofu, and top with fresh parsley and enjoy!

Vegan Sloppy Joes

Preparation time: 15 minutes

Cook time: 45 minutes

Total time: 60 minutes

Servings: 2

Ingredients:

- ¼ cup of green/brown lentils
- ¼ cup of red lentils
- ½ cup of water
- 7 oz. canned crushed tomatoes (We love the Muir Glen Fire Roasted variety)
- 1 tbsp. of tomato paste
- ½ tbsp. of Vegan Worcestershire sauce (We love The Wizard's brand or Annie's Naturals)
- ¼ tsp. of salt
- ¼ tbsp. of ground cumin
- ¼ tsp. of dried oregano
- ¼ large onion, chopped
- ¼ sweet bell pepper or poblano pepper, chopped
- ¼ tbsp. of olive oil or grapeseed oil, optional
- ½ tbsp. of apple cider vinegar
- ½ tbsp. of maple syrup, optional
- ¼ cup of Vegan Ground Beef, optional

Cooking Instructions:

1. Press the Sauté function on your Instant Pot and add the onion, salt, and bell pepper. Sauté the ingredients for about minutes.
2. Add the cumin and oregano and sauté for 1 minute. Add the tomato paste and give everything a good stir to coat. Sauté for additional 1 to 2 minutes.
3. Add the rest of the ingredients and stir again. Close and lock the lid in place. Select Manual, High Pressure for 13 minutes.
4. When the timer beeps, do a natural pressure release for about 10 minutes. Carefully remove the lid and stir in the vegan ground beef, if desired.
5. Serve over toasted hamburger buns and enjoy!

Cilantro Lime Quinoa

Servings: 2

Preparation time: 5 minutes

Cook time: 30 minutes

Total time: 35 minutes

Ingredients:

- 1.5 ounce of green chili
- ¼ onion, roughly chopped
- ¼ bunch cilantro
- ½ cup of quinoa
- ¾ teaspoon of veggie bouillon
- 1 cloves garlic, minced
- ½ cups of water
- Juice of half lime
- Salt & pepper to taste

Cooking Instructions:

1. Add together the green chili, onion, and cilantro in a food processor or blender and until smooth.
2. Add the blended mixture and rest of the ingredients except for the lime juice into the bottom of your Instant Pot.
3. Close and lock the lid in place. Select Manual, High Pressure for 5 minutes. When the timer beeps, do a natural pressure release for about 10 minutes.
4. Carefully remove the lid and fluff quinoa and mix in lime juice. Serve and enjoy!

Vegan Alfredo Sauce

Preparation time: 10 minutes

Cook time: 3 minutes

Total time: 13 minutes

Servings: 2

Calories: 110 kcal

Ingredients:

- 0.67 tbsp. of olive oil
- 2.67 cloves garlic, minced
- 2 cups of cauliflower florets (fresh or frozen)
- 0.25 cup of raw cashews
- 1 cup of vegetable broth
- 0.17-0.33 tsp. of salt, to taste
- 0.33 l. of cooked fettuccine pasta (whole grain or gluten free if needed)
- Steamed broccoli, kale or green peas, optional

Cooking Instructions:

1. Press the Sauté function on your Instant Pot and add the olive oil. Add the minced garlic and sauté for about 1 to 2 minutes or until fragrant.
2. Press the Cancel function. Add the cauliflower, cashews and vegetable broth. Close and lock the lid in place. Select Manual, High Pressure for 3 minutes.
3. When the timer beeps, do a quick pressure release. Carefully remove the lid and pour to a blender. Add salt and blend until very smooth.
4. Pour over pasta and give everything a good stir. Add a couple tablespoons of water if the sauce is too thick, until your desired consistency is achieved.
5. Serve with steamed broccoli, kale or peas if desired.

Maple Bourbon Chili

Preparation time: 10 minutes

Cook time: 10 minutes

Total time: 10 minutes

Servings: 2

Calories: 239 kcal

Ingredients:

- 0.5 tablespoon of cooking oil
- 0.5 medium yellow onion, thinly sliced
- 1-1.5 cloves garlic, minced
- 2 cups of sweet potatoes, peeled and cubed into 1/2" pieces
- 1 cup of vegetable broth
- 0.75 tablespoon of chili powder
- 1 teaspoon of cumin
- 0.25 teaspoon of paprika
- 0.13 teaspoon of cayenne pepper
- 1 (15) oz. cans kidney beans, drained and rinsed
- 0.5 (15) oz. can diced tomatoes
- 0.13 cup of bourbon
- 1 tablespoon of maple syrup
- Salt and pepper, to taste
- A few fresh springs of cilantro
- 1 green onions, diced

- 1.5 small corn tortillas, toasted and sliced, optional

Cooking Instructions:

1. Press the Sauté function on your Instant Pot and add the cooking oil. Once hot, add the onions and cook for about 5 minutes, stirring occasionally, until onions are soft.
2. Add the garlic and cook for additional 30 seconds. Add the cubed sweet potatoes, chili powder, cumin, paprika, and cayenne pepper, and give everything a good stir to coat the vegetables.
3. Add the vegetable broth, beans, tomatoes, maple syrup, and bourbon. Close and lock the lid in place. Select the Soup function and adjust to cook for 15 minutes.
4. When the timer beeps, do a quick pressure release. Carefully open the lid and check the sweet potatoes to ensure that they are tender.
5. If you desire to use tortillas, lightly oil a cast iron skillet and pan fry the tortillas on per side for about 2-3 minutes or until crispy.
6. Transfer the tortillas to a bowl and allow to cool for a couple of minutes. Cut them into thin strips. Serve with cilantro, green onions, and toasted tortillas.

Vegan Mashed Potatoes

Preparation time: 10 minutes

Cook time: 20 minutes

Total time: 30 minutes

Servings: 2

Calories: 98 kcal

Ingredients:

- 1.67 - 2 potatoes, cubed into large pieces Yukon gold or baking potatoes, peeled
- 1.67 cloves of garlic
- 0.17 teaspoon of salt
- 0.33 tablespoon of extra virgin olive oil or vegan butter
- A good dash of black pepper
- A dash of parsley or thyme
- A pinch of nutmeg
- 0.33 cup full fat coconut milk
- Fresh chives for garnish

Cooking Instructions:

1. Add the cubed potatoes, garlic cloves, 0.17 teaspoon of salt along with 1 cup of water into the bottom of your Instant Pot.
2. Close and lock the lid in place. Select Manual, High Pressure for 4 minutes. When the timer beeps, do a quick pressure release. Carefully open the lid.
3. Add the potatoes into a large pot, and pour enough water to cover them. Bring to a boil and cook for about 10-15 mins, or until they are tender.
4. Transfer to a colander to drain. Add them to a bowl and allow them sit for a couple of minutes to dry out. Mash lightly and allow to sit for the steam to escape.
5. Mash the cooked garlic and mix in salt, the remaining ingredients and half cup coconut milk. Mix and whip lightly and allow to sit for about 1 minutes for the milks to incorporate and absorb.

6. Adjust the seasoning with more salt and pepper. Add more coconut milk until your creamier consistency is reached. Garnish with chives.
7. Serve hot with gravy and enjoy!

DESSERT MEALS

Applesauce

Preparation time: 30 minutes

Cook time: 5 minutes

Total time: 35 minutes

Serves: 2

Ingredients:

- 2 ½ lb. of fresh apples, remove the cores and chop into quarters
- Juice of ½ lemon
- 1 cinnamon stick
- A pinch of pink salt
- ¼ cup of water
- 1 small red beet, peeled and chopped into 6 pieces, optional
- Honey to taste, optional

Cooking Instructions:

1. Add the chopped apples into the bottom of your Instant Pot and squeeze the lemon juice on top. Add the cinnamon stick, salt and water.
2. Give everything a good stir it a gentle stir. Add the chopped beet. Close and lock the lid in place. Select Manual, High Pressure for 5 minutes.
3. When the timer beeps, do a natural pressure release for about 15 minutes. Carefully remove the lid and remove the cinnamon stick.
4. Puree the ingredients in an immersion blender or blender until smooth. Ladle into individual bowls.
5. Serve and enjoy!

Buttered Cabbage

Preparation time: 10 minutes

Cook time: 6 minutes

Total time: 16 minutes

Servings: 2

Calories: 263kcal

Ingredients:

- 0.5 head of cabbage chopped into 1 inch pieces
- 0.25 cup of butter unsalted
- 0.5 cup of chicken broth
- Salt & fresh ground pepper

Cooking Instructions:

1. Add the chicken broth and butter into the bottom of your Instant Pot. Place the chopped cabbage on top.
2. Close and lock the lid in place. Select Manual, High Pressure for 6 minutes. When the timer beeps, do a quick pressure release.
3. Carefully remove the lid and stir the cabbage. Adjust the seasoning with salt and fresh ground pepper to taste.
4. Serve and enjoy!

Egg Bites

Preparation time: 10 minutes

Cook time: 19 minutes

Total time: 29 minutes

Servings: 2

Calories: 366.6kcal

Ingredients:

- 2 large eggs
- 2 pieces of bacon, cooked and crumbled
- 0.75 cup of sharp cheddar cheese, shredded
- 0.25 cup of cottage cheese
- 0.13 cup of heavy cream
- 0.5 teaspoon of hot sauce
- 0.13 cup of spinach, chopped
- Salt & pepper to taste

Cooking Instructions:

1. Place pieces of bacon into silicone baby food maker in the molds and keep aside.
2. In your blender, add the eggs, cheddar cheese, cottage cheese, heavy cream, hot sauce, and salt and pepper and blend until smooth consistency.
3. Stir in chopped spinach. Pour egg mixture into baby silicone baby food maker and cover the bacon with a piece of aluminum foil.
4. Pour 1 cup of water into the bottom of your Instant Pot and place the trivet. Add the baby food maker on top of trivet.
5. Close and lock the lid in place. Select the Steam function and adjust to cook for 9 minutes. When the timer beeps, do a natural pressure release for about 10 minutes, the quick release any remaining pressure.
6. Carefully remove the lid remove the silicone baby maker. Allow to sit for a couple of minutes and turn eggs over onto a dish. Serve immediately and enjoy!

Carrot Cake Cheesecake

Preparation time: 15 minutes

Cook time: 35 minutes

Total time: 50 minutes

Servings: 2

Calories: 818kcal

Ingredients:

For the Cheesecake:

- 4 ounces of cream cheese softened
- 0.25 cup of granulated sugar
- 1 tablespoon of sour cream
- 0.5 tablespoon of all-purpose flour
- 0.5 large egg
- 0.5 teaspoon of vanilla extract

For the Carrot Cake:

- 0.25 cup of vegetable oil
- 0.25 cup of granulated sugar
- 0.25 cup of flour
- 0.25 teaspoon of baking soda
- 0.25 teaspoon of cinnamon
- 0.13 teaspoon of nutmeg
- Pinch of salt
- 0.5 large egg

- 0.5 teaspoon of vanilla
- 0.13 cup of crushed pineapple drained
- 0.5 cup of grated carrot
- 0.13 cup of walnuts, chopped

Cooking Instructions:

1. Grease a 7 inch spring form pan, and set aside. In a medium bowl, add together the cream cheese, sugar, sour cream, and flour to make the cheesecake batter.
2. Use a hand mixer and beat on medium speed until smooth. Add the egg and vanilla and continue beating until blended and set aside.
3. In a separate bowl, add the vegetable oil and sugar. Use a hand mixer and beat on medium speed until blended. Add together the flour, baking soda, cinnamon, nutmeg, and salt, egg, and vanilla extract.
4. Beat on medium speed until well blended. Add the carrots, pineapple, and walnuts and fold the mixture into batter with a spatula.
5. Pour half of the carrot cake mixture into the greased spring form pan and spread it to cover the bottom of the pan.
6. Add the cream cheese batter in the center of the carrot cake batter. Gently spread the cream cheese mixture over the cake mixture.
7. Repeat the same procedure with the remaining ingredients until all batter fills the spring form pan, and place the cream cheese layer on top.
8. Cover the spring form pan with a piece of aluminum foil. Pour 1 cup of water into the bottom of your Instant Pot and place the trivet inside. Add the cake on trivet.
9. Close and lock the lid in place. Select Manual, High Pressure for 35 minutes. When the timer beeps, do a natural pressure release for about 10 minutes.
10. Carefully open the lid and transfer the cake to cool on a counter. Refrigerate for at least 6 to 24 hours.
11. Serve and enjoy!

Garlic Noodles

Preparation time: 15 minutes

Cook time: 6 minutes

Total time: 21 minutes

Servings: 2

Calories: 250kcal

Ingredients:

- 0.5 cup of water
- 0.5 cup of chicken broth
- 3 cloves garlic, minced
- 1 tablespoon of soy sauce
- 1 tablespoon of brown sugar
- 0.5 tablespoon of oyster sauce
- 0.5 teaspoon of sesame oil
- 0.5 teaspoon of chili paste (Sambal Oelek}
- 4 ounces of thin spaghetti noodles, broken in half
- Sesame seeds, for topping
- Green onion, for topping

Cooking Instructions:

1. Add together the water, chicken broth, garlic, soy sauce, brown sugar, oyster sauce, sesame oil, and chili paste into the bottom of your Instant Pot.
2. Give everything a good whisk to incorporate. Add the broken spaghetti noodles on top, and ensure that they are covered with the cooking liquid.
3. Close and lock the lid in place. Select Manual, High Pressure for 6 minutes. When the timer beeps, do a quick pressure release.

4. Carefully remove the lid and stir the pasta noodles, allowing the noodles to separate and the sauce to thicken. Ladle into serving bowls.
5. Top with sesame seeds and green onions if desired. Serve and enjoy!

Arroz Con Leche

Preparation time: 5 minutes

Cook time: 20 minutes

Total time: 35 minutes

Serves: 2

Ingredients:

For the Rice:

- 1 cup of white, long grain rice
- 1 ¼ cups of water
- 2 cups of whole milk
- ⅛ teaspoon of salt

Add after Cooking:

- 1 can sweetened condensed milk, 14 ounces
- 1 teaspoon of vanilla extract
- Cinnamon, for topping

Cooking Instructions:

1. Add the rice in a mesh strainer and rinse until the water runs clean.
2. Add the milk, water, rice and salt into the bottom of your Instant Pot and give everything a good stir.
3. Close and lock the lid in place. Select the Porridge function and adjust to cook for 20 minutes.
4. When the timer beeps, do a natural pressure release for about 10 minutes, then quick release any remaining pressure.
5. Carefully remove the lid and add the can of condensed milk and the teaspoon of vanilla extract to the rice. Give everything a good mix.
6. Serve warm and enjoy!

Apple Cake

Preparation time: 20 minutes

Cook time: 1 hour

Total time: 1 hour 20 minutes

Servings: 2

Calories: 275 kcal

Ingredients:

- 0.75 cup of peeled and diced apples into small pieces, any variety
- 0.13 tbsp. of ground cinnamon
- 0.5 tbsp. of sugar
- 0.25-0.13 cup of flour + 1 tbsp. of for dusting the pan
- 0.13 tbsp. of baking powder
- 0.13 tsp. of fine sea salt
- 0.13 cup of vegetable oil
- 0.19 cup of sugar
- 0.5 tbsp. of orange juice
- 0.25 tsp. of vanilla extract
- 0.5 large eggs, room temperature

Cooking Instructions:

1. Grease and flour a 7-inch cake pan. Toss with cinnamon and 0.5 tbsp. of sugar and set aside. In a medium bowl, mix the flour, baking powder and salt and set aside.
2. In another bowl, whisk together the oil, orange juice, sugar, vanilla and eggs. Add the wet ingredients into dry ingredients and give everything a good mix until incorporated.
3. Pour half of batter in the cake pan. Spread half of apples on top of the batter. Gently pour the rest of the batter to cover most of the apple pieces.

4. Spread the rest of the apples and any juices on top. Cover the cake pan with a piece of aluminum foil. Pour 1 cup of water into the bottom of your Instant Pot and place the trivet inside.
5. Close and lock the lid in place. Select Manual, High Pressure for about 60 minutes. When the timer beeps, do a natural pressure release for about 10 minutes.
6. Carefully remove the lid and remove the trivet. Remove the aluminum foil. Place the cake on a wire rack to cool. Serve and enjoy!

Pumpkin Pie Pudding

Preparation time: 10 minutes

Cook time: 30 minutes

Total time: 40 minutes

Servings: 2

Calories: 184 kcal

Ingredients:

- 0.67 eggs
- 0.17 cup of heavy whipping cream or almond milk
- 0.25 cup of Erythritol (sub Swerve, Truvia, Splenda or sweetener of choice)
- 5 oz. canned pumpkin puree
- 0.33 tsp. of pumpkin pie spice
- 0.33 tsp. of vanilla
- 0.17 cup of heavy whipping cream, for finishing

Cooking Instructions:

1. In a medium bowl, whisk together the egg and add the remaining ingredients. Grease a 6-inch x 3-inch pan with a silicone basting brush.
2. Pour the mixture into the pan. Pour 1 cup of water into the bottom of your Instant Pot and place the steamer rack.
3. Place the pan with the pumpkin mixture on the rack. Cover the pan with a piece of aluminum foil. Close and lock the lid in place.
4. Select Manual, High Pressure for 20 minutes. When the timer beeps, do a natural pressure release for about 10 minutes.
5. Carefully remove the lid and remove the pan. Refrigerate for at least 6 to 8 hours. Serve with more whipped cream and enjoy!